RADIANT FAITH

Also by M.J. Fievre

For Teens

Badass Black Girl
Empowered Black Girl
Resilient Black Girl
Black and Resilient
Walk Boldly
Female, Gifted, and Black
Black Brave Beautiful
The Book of Awesome Black Women
The Ultimate Book of Confidence for Teen Girls

For Adults

Raising Confident Black Kids
Happy, Okay?

For Kids

A Cat Named Sam
Haiti A to Z
Young Trailblazers: The Book of Black Inventors and Scientists
The Ocean Lives There
Young Trailblazers: The Book of Black Heroes and Groundbreakers

RADIANT FAITH

A 52-Week Devotional Journey for Teen Girls

MJ Fievre

CORAL GABLES

For permission requests, please contact the publisher at:
Mango Publishing Group
2850 S Douglas Road, 2nd Floor
Coral Gables, FL 33134 USA
info@mango.bz

For special orders, quantity sales, course adoptions and corporate sales, please email the publisher at sales@mango.bz. For trade and wholesale sales, please contact Ingram Publisher Services at customer.service@ingramcontent.com or +1.800.509.4887.

Radiant Faith: A 52-Week Devotional Journey for Teen Girls

Library of Congress Cataloging-in-Publication number: 2023945348
ISBN: (pb) 978-1-68481-393-3, (hc) 978-1-68481-394-0,
(e) 978-1-68481-395-7
BISAC category code: YAN048020, YOUNG ADULT NONFICTION / Religious / Christian / Devotional & Prayer

*To my Freedom sisters: Chantel, Yaya, Natalie B.,
Natalie R., Melissa, Nichole, and Ruth*

*Thank you for seeing me and allowing
me to be vulnerable*

Contents

Introduction: Hey There!   9

Week 1: Embrace Your Identity in God   12

Week 2: Build Self-Worth and Confidence   17

Week 3: Navigate Friendships Gracefully   23

Week 4: Cultivate a Strong Prayer Life   28

Week 5: Discover Your Spiritual Gifts   32

Week 6: Overcome Fear and Anxiety   37

Week 7: Embrace the Power of Forgiveness   41

Week 8: Develop a Servant's Heart   46

Week 9: Honor Your Parents and Guardians   50

Week 10: Manage Stress and Time   54

Week 11: Build Healthy Relationships   59

Week 12: Find Your Purpose and Calling   64

Week 13: Balance School, Work, and Faith   68

Week 14: Make Wise Choices   72

Week 15: Cultivate Gratitude   76

Week 16: Grow in Your Faith Journey   80

Week 17: Understand God's Love   85

Week 18: Live with Integrity   89

Week 19: Encourage Others   94

Week 20: Be a Light in the World   98

Week 21: Practice Contentment   103

Week 22: Deal with Doubt   108

Week 23: Set Boundaries   113

Week 24: Overcome Temptation   118

Week 25: Learn from the Strength and Faith of Esther   123

Week 26: Develop a Heart for Worship   128

Week 27: Practice Patience   132

Week 28: Prioritize Spiritual Growth   137

Week 29: Trust in God's Timing   141

Week 30: Learn from Mistakes   146

Week 31: Stay Connected to God's Love   150

Week 32: Embrace Change   155

Week 33: Lean on God in Times of Need   160

Week 34: Pursue a Life of Humility   164

Week 35: Cultivate a Heart of Compassion   169

Week 36: Strengthen Your Faith Community   174

Week 37: Be a Good Steward   178

Week 38: Let Go of Control   183

Week 39: Walk in Obedience   187

Week 40: Live Out Your Faith Boldly   191

Week 41: Find Joy in the Journey   196

Week 42: Embrace Rest   200

Week 43: Pray for Others   205

Week 44: Build Unity in Diversity   210

Week 45: Learn to Listen   215

Week 46: Overcome Discouragement   219

Week 47: Stand Firm in Your Convictions   223

Week 48: Believe in the Power of Testimony   228

Week 49: Share Your Faith with Others   233

Week 50: Invest in Eternity   238

Week 51: Celebrate God's Faithfulness   243

Week 52: Step into Your Future with Confidence   248

Conclusion: What a Ride It's Been!   252

About the Author   254

Introduction:
Hey There!

First off, major props to you for picking up *Radiant Faith*. Consider this your compass for the upcoming year, guiding vibrant souls like yourself through the rollercoaster of life. Over the next fifty-two weeks, you'll uncover insights, stories, and wisdom that touch on everything from embracing your unique identity in God to navigating the intricate web of friendships, dreams, and self-discovery.

Picture this: a young girl growing up in Haiti, surrounded by both the vibrancy of her homeland and the violence that often threatened its pulse. That was me, growing up in the buzzing streets of Port-au-Prince. But often, chaos broke out. Home was no different. The walls of our home, while keeping out the city's noise, also bore witness to our family's fights. Life was a loud mixture of music and mayhem. And like many, I often grappled with a burning question: "Why?"

My faith became my sanctuary in those turbulent times. Within the walls of my high school, Sainte Rose de Lima, the teachings of the Bible provided me with solace and an anchor. Under the tutelage of Sister Anne-Marie, I became one of the leaders of Jeunesse Mariale, a Marian youth movement dedicated to fostering faith and devotion among young believers. I then had the privilege of mentoring my peers. With our shared faith, we found hope and a sense of purpose even as chaos unfolded around us. Through Jeunesse Mariale, I listened to my peers' many heartfelt stories of resilience and faith—stories I adapted and shared in this book. We strengthened our bond when the youth group journeyed to Italy and France for the Catholic Charismatic Renewal in 2000. These travels exposed me to narratives that enriched my understanding and appreciation of the bond faith can create among individuals; they inspired many of the stories that breathe life into this book.

At Université Notre Dame in Haiti, my academic journey turned toward a profound exploration of faith. Studying under Father Elder, I immersed myself in theological studies, diving into the nuances of biblical texts, ancient religious traditions, and contemporary interpretations of Christianity. This environment cultivated my curiosity and critical thinking, pushing me to question, reflect, and grow spiritually. Later, when I transitioned to Barry University in Miami Shores, the multicultural backdrop of the institution broadened my perspective even further. There, I encountered diverse voices and beliefs, which challenged and enriched my understanding of Christianity in a global context. Throughout both educational experiences, my passion for faith remained steadfast, driving me to relentlessly seek knowledge and answers at the very heart of Christianity.

As a teenager and young adult, I was a cyclone. I won't pretend I always had it together. There were moments during the tumult of home and heart when I felt myself splintering, and my pain spilled over, hurting those around me. I lied, cheated, and inflicted pain—yet paradoxically, I also loved, supported, and uplifted. Here's the truth: my actions, born from brokenness, affected those around me. Yet, in those very fractures, my faith shone brightest, mending me, and making me whole again. Through those shards of chaos and hurt, my faith emerged, resilient. It gave me the strength to face each dawn, to hope, and to believe, even when circumstances screamed otherwise, guiding me to hope in a sea of doubt.

Today, having journeyed from the vibrant streets of South Florida, I call Winter Garden my home. I've found peace and purpose here with my loving husband, Thomas. Through my baptism at Hope Church—a profound, heartful commitment—I've grown closer to God, guided by the unwavering spirit of our pastors, Wesley Beacham and Diana Janney Beacham.

In *Radiant Faith*, I share the core lessons and moments from my journey—seeking answers, embracing hope, and bathing in a love that never wavers, even when faced with the harshest storms. Through this guide, I hope you find strength, resilience, and a radiant faith that lights up even the darkest paths.

Are you new to faith? Great! Been walking with God for a while now? Awesome! Wherever you stand on your spiritual path, *Radiant Faith* is here to jazz up your journey. I've filled these pages with tales of perseverance, candid reflections on challenges, and encouragement to help you overcome obstacles. Because here's the truth: God has some seriously cool plans for you. And I want to help you uncover more of that divine blueprint every week.

Every segment in this guide includes a mix of soulful scriptures, relatable tales, and actionable nuggets to help you build that rock-solid confidence and find your groove in life. The goal? To help you anchor yourself in God's unwavering love, especially when it feels like life's playlist is on shuffle.

I hope *Radiant Faith* becomes your go-to companion—the book you scribble notes in, dog-ear pages, and revisit when you need a faith-filled pep talk. Ready to dive deep? Let's grow, laugh, question, and discover with *Radiant Faith*. Fasten your seatbelt. Adventure awaits!

Let's take this journey together, and embrace every challenge, every joy, every moment of doubt, and every revelation. Here you go!

With all my heart,
M.J. Fievre

Week 1: Embrace Your Identity in God

*"Before I formed you in the womb I knew you,
before you were born I set you apart."*
—Jeremiah 1:5

Recommended Reading:
The story of David and Goliath (1 Samuel 17)

It's tempting to define yourself by the views and likes on social media. But here's some real talk: you're worth so much more. Your identity is rooted in how God sees you, not how the world sees you. Like Jeremiah's affirmation that God recognized and esteemed you even before birth, your true self is eternal and immutable. I hope you uncover layers of your identity and their deep ties to God this week.

God crafted you with a specific vision. That's the thrill—there's nobody else in the world just like you! Embracing this realization is the secret to shaking off external pressures. In the Bible, you'll often see that those who understood their divine identity stood out and made a difference. And the first steps? Dive deep into prayer and scripture, and build connections with other uplifting, faith-driven teens.

David's face-off with Goliath in First Samuel is an inspiring tale of self-worth. David, the youngest and often overlooked boy, knew his worth not from the world but from God. He internalized the very essence of Jeremiah's words, recognizing that his true identity lay in his relationship with the Divine. When Goliath, the Philistine giant, taunted the Israelites, everyone hesitated except David. Despite King Saul's reservations about his young age, David was unwavering. He recounted his victories over a lion and a bear, attributing them to God: "The Lord who rescued me from the paw of the lion and the paw of the bear will rescue me from the hand of this Philistine" (1 Samuel 17:34–37).

With just a sling and five stones, David confronted Goliath. And with a precise shot, he defeated Goliath. This victory wasn't just David's; it was a win for everyone who knew their worth in God's eyes. It echoed the profound message of Jeremiah, proving that your divine identity is a source of unparalleled strength.

Your True Self

Ever felt like the world's trying to put you into a box? Between the rush for likes, the race for views, and the urge to trend on social media, it sometimes feels like you're always chasing an elusive mold. Ever thought, "Is this truly me?" Your identity isn't defined by trends or peers. It's anchored in God, who designed you with precision and love, like a passionate artist. And once you truly grasp this? You'll experience the exhilaration of authentic living.

Rising Above

Nathalie had always been good at science. It was a simple fact, like how the sun rises or how fish swim. One day, the school picked her to lead a science project—a model for a green city. Important. Potentially national science fair material.

But in the echo of the school's empty corridors, she heard it. A whisper, sharp as the sting of a bee. "Why Nathalie? Sarah's better for this," they said. The words settled heavily in her chest.

That evening, a glass of water in her hand, she caught her own eyes in the window's reflection. Doubt stared back. Just then, a gust of wind blew an old card off her bedside table. It read, Psalm 139:14: "I praise you because I am fearfully and wonderfully made." The passage echoed the message of Jeremiah, emphasizing that God's design and purpose for us is unique and special. The words weren't just comforting; they were empowering. She wasn't just Nathalie, the student; she was Nathalie, the innovator, the problem solver. She considered the verse for a moment, then started sketching.

With renewed vigor, she used her faith as a foundation for her actions. The following weeks were methodical. Nathalie made plans; she implemented changes. The prototype emerged—solar designs, recycled materials. The project became a testament to the beauty of simple, sustainable living. Nathalie displayed divine craftsmanship through her work, just as Jeremiah had declared.

The day came. The school gathered. Nathalie presented, each word measured, each fact irrefutable. With the prototype on display, Nathalie passionately explained its features and benefits. She discussed rainwater collection, solar panels, and green spaces designed for urban settings. The murmurs faded. The applause afterward felt like a roaring ocean. Even the whispering girls stood, looking at Nathalie's project with newfound respect.

But for Nathalie, it was never about the crowd. It was about the quiet resolve, the work, the understanding that she had a place in the world, and it was right where she stood. She faced doubt, leaned on her faith, and emerged stronger. Her journey mirrored David's, showcasing that your connection with God is an unbreakable rope to your true self.

Because, at the end of the day, it's not about what others think, but how you rise above and find your rhythm.

Daily Dose of Faith

Jeremiah reminds you of your unique creation even before your birth. Want to harness authenticity?

* **Dive into the Bible:** Embrace scriptures that resonate with you and let them guide your days.

* **Build Your Tribe:** Seek friends who elevate your faith rather than drench you in negativity.

* **Reflect:** A journal (or even your phone's notes app) can be a haven. Ponder on scriptures, and see their influence in your daily encounters. Pen down your emotions and see the magic.

Living the Faith

Living in faith means understanding that you have a designated purpose meticulously crafted by the Creator. Own your identity in God! Remember David. He looked like an underdog, yet he defeated Goliath. Drawing strength from his deep-seated belief in his God-given worth, he knew his worth in God's eyes, and with that belief, you, too, can face any challenge.

Journal Time!

* Reflect on a moment when you felt out of place. How did you feel? Did you feel distanced from your divine identity? Knowing what you do now, what advice would you give your younger self?

* What's a quirky trait you possess? How can you view it as God's special touch in creating you? Think about how this trait might mirror a specific purpose God has for you.

* What would it say if God sent you a direct message expressing how He sees you? Would it echo Jeremiah's words, reminding you of your unique creation and purpose?

Wrapping Up the Week

As you move through the week, never forget: you're not just a face in a vast crowd. Crafted with divine precision, you are a unique masterpiece, born from the love and intentionality of the Creator, a testament to God's unmatched artistry.

Week 2: Build Self-Worth and Confidence

"I can do all things through Christ who strengthens me."
—Philippians 4:13

Recommended Reading:
The story of Deborah (Judges 4 and 5)

Everyone's buzzing about "self-worth" and "confidence," but the road to truly understanding these words is one epic journey. You live in a world that constantly tells you that you're not enough. But guess what? God sees you differently. You can learn the divine truth about your worth and confidence. You can draw strength and confidence from Christ, reaffirming your self-worth in Him.

Scripture is filled with stories of women who exemplify empowerment and divine purpose. Their tales echo a timeless truth: that your self-worth is inherent, given by God. These tales teach you that no matter your background or society's expectations, God's plans and your self-worth are deeply intertwined.

Deborah, a prophetess, was the only female judge mentioned in the Bible. In a time dominated by male leaders, she stood out as a pillar of strength, wisdom, and inspiration. Israel was facing oppression from the Canaanite King Jabin.

Under Deborah's leadership and direction, Barak led the Israelites into battle. With her prophecy and encouragement, Barak and the Israelites achieved a stunning victory over their oppressors.

Deborah's faith, coupled with her understanding of her divine role, led her people to freedom. Her story emphasizes that when you recognize your God-given worth and purpose, you can rise above societal constraints.

Your True Self

Despite societal constraints, Deborah grasped her divine purpose, showcasing that her leadership was not just a position, but a reflection of her understanding of her worth in God's grand plan. Through her, you can learn the power of confidence grounded in divine purpose. Even in a patriarchal society, Deborah's confidence in her purpose shone as a light of hope.

Isn't it a tad crazy that with billions of people in the world, there's only one *you*? This distinctiveness is God's signature on your life. Getting caught up in the comparison game is easy—grades, sports, followers, or fashion. Flip the script. Instead of trying to fit into someone else's shoes, recognize that your pair, designed by God Himself, fits perfectly. The spotlight shouldn't be on what you lack, but on celebrating what you have.

Luminous Strokes

At Jericho High, Alex was the golden girl—the captain of the cheerleading squad and an honor roll student. Jenny, her sixteen-year-old sister, was mostly referred to as "Alex's younger sister."

But in the quiet of her room, surrounded by a world of color and sketches, Jenny came alive. The rustling pages and the swish of her brushes were her sanctuary. Here, she wasn't in Alex's shadow but in the embrace of her own luminous world. Just like Deborah found her strength in God, Jenny found hers in God's gift: the strokes of her brush.

One afternoon, after a particularly grueling math test, Jenny found a note in her sketchbook. It read: "See me after class.—Mrs. Harris." The heartbeats in Jenny's chest quickened. She couldn't recall doing anything wrong in her art class.

After school, she approached Mrs. Harris's classroom with trepidation. The familiar smell of paint and turpentine greeted her. "Jenny," Mrs. Harris began, "I hope you're not mad, but I entered one of your sketches in the Statewide Youth Art Contest."

Jenny was taken aback. "You did what?"

Mrs. Harris handed her a brochure. On the cover was Jenny's sketch: a delicate rendition of an old oak tree from the schoolyard. The light filtered through its leaves, casting dappled shadows. It was a moment Jenny had captured during a lonely lunch, feeling overshadowed by Alex's achievements.

"A week ago," Mrs. Harris continued, "I received the results." She paused, letting the tension build, then grinned. "You won, Jenny. First place."

Jenny felt a rush of emotions—disbelief, gratitude, and an overwhelming sense of validation. Her hands trembled as she held the brochure. A small award ceremony was scheduled for the following week.

The day arrived faster than Jenny could process it. The school auditorium was abuzz with chatter, but for the first time, it wasn't about Alex. It was about Jenny's art.

As she stepped on stage to receive her award, she spotted Alex in the crowd. Her sister was beaming with pride, her eyes shining bright.

But what struck Jenny most was a newfound respect in Alex's gaze. They were no longer just the popular girl and her overshadowed sister; they were two individuals, each with their own talent and worth. Through her journey, Jenny embraced the Philippians 4:13 truth: with Christ, she could achieve all things. She saw her potential through God's lens; she realized her worth.

In the weeks that followed, Jenny's sketches garnered more attention. Students approached her for custom pieces, and teachers applauded her talent. Jenny's journey underscores the transformative power of self-worth and divine guidance. Her most significant change was internal. Jenny painted her story with each brush stroke, understanding that everyone has their spotlight, waiting for the right moment to shine.

As Jenny added the award to her art corner, she took a moment to reflect. It wasn't the accolade that mattered most; it was the realization that followed. She didn't have to walk in Alex's shadow or mimic her path. She had her own journey, one that was unique and divinely crafted.

Daily Dose of Faith

Self-worth isn't just a one-time achievement. As you learn from Deborah, it's an ongoing journey of faith and understanding. It's like a favorite song on repeat. Much like Deborah experienced, it's the affirmation that God values and believes in you. Your actions, words, and thoughts align when you truly believe in your divine worth. You no longer hustle for approval; instead, you radiate confidence, not from vanity but from a deep-rooted belief in God's love for you.

*   **Mirror Talk:** Look in the mirror every morning and say something positive about yourself.

*   **Positive Vibes Only:** Steer clear of negativity. Surround yourself with uplifting friends, music, and media.

*   **Skill Up:** Is there something you're passionate about? Dive in deeper! Whether it's painting, writing, or coding, make time for it.

Living the Faith

Stories like that of Deborah are timeless reminders of your potential and God's plan in your life. Deborah's confidence stemmed from her unwavering faith. By recognizing God's hand in their stories, Deborah and Jenny could redefine their self-worth in a world of expectations. You can find confidence and purpose in your path by embracing your unique gifts and roles.

Journal Time!

* Reflect on a time you felt overshadowed or underestimated. How did it feel, and how did you overcome it? Dive deep into that moment. Recall the emotions, surroundings, and internal dialogue. Then, think about how God might have been guiding you through that experience. Perhaps, like Deborah, He was preparing you for something bigger.

* Write about a talent or quality you have but tend to undervalue. You have gifts, some of which you might not recognize or appreciate fully. Describe one of these qualities or talents. What makes it unique? And how can you use it for a greater purpose? Connect this to how Deborah utilized her leadership skills at a time when women leaders were scarce.

* If God were to give you a pep talk right now, what would He say? Imagine sitting across from Him, listening intently. What words of encouragement, guidance, or love would He share with you? He sees your full potential, much like He saw Deborah's. Allow this exercise to bring comfort, motivation, and a renewed sense of purpose.

Wrapping Up the Week

As you come to the end of this week, remember: your worth is not determined by society's standards, peer opinions, or even self-imposed expectations. As beautifully illustrated in the story of Deborah, and even Jenny, your worth is divinely ordained. It is unchangeable, eternal, and deeply rooted in God's love for you.

Every time you doubt your worth or feel overshadowed, envision a loving God cheering you on, whispering words of encouragement. Embrace the truth that "With God on our side, who can be against us?" (Romans 8:31). ("You got this because I got you!") Hold onto that unwavering faith, let it be your guiding light, and march confidently into the days ahead. With your unique talents and story, you have a distinct place in God's divine plan.

Week 3: Navigate Friendships Gracefully

"Do not be misled: Bad company corrupts good character."
–1 Corinthians 15:33

Recommended Reading:
The story of Naomi and Ruth (Book of Ruth)

Friendships offer unexpected turns and lessons. They have ups and downs, doubt, joy, and resilience. Like the bond between Naomi and Ruth, friendships can teach us loyalty and steadfastness. And while friendships might seem like rollercoaster rides, they lay the foundation for bonds that could last a lifetime. Faith and understanding can help navigate these intricacies.

The steadfast bond between Naomi and Ruth in the Bible echoes the complexities and beauties of friendships. Naomi, an Israelite, and her family moved from Bethlehem to Moab due to a famine. In Moab, her two sons married Moabite women, one of whom was Ruth. Unfortunately, tragedy struck Naomi when she lost her husband and her two sons. Left in a foreign land with her two daughters-in-law, Naomi decided to return to Bethlehem. She urged her daughters-in-law to return to their families so that they could have a chance at a better life. Orpah, one of them, tearfully went back. But Ruth made a heart-moving declaration of loyalty: "Do not urge me to leave you or to return from following you. For where you go, I will go, and where you lodge, I will lodge. Your people shall be my people, and your God my God" (Ruth 1:16).

This unwavering commitment seen in Ruth's words is the very essence that friendships should strive for in today's world. Ruth's commitment to Naomi wasn't just out of duty as a daughter-in-law but out of genuine love and companionship. She left her homeland, people, and gods to stand by Naomi's side.

Upon returning to Bethlehem, Ruth faced challenges as a foreigner. But her loyalty to Naomi and her hard work in the fields caught the attention of Boaz, a kind and wealthy landowner. Boaz and Ruth's eventual marriage ensured the well-being of the widowed Naomi, illustrating how Ruth's decision to stay with Naomi led to blessings for them both.

Their story showcases the selflessness, loyalty, and strength inherent in true friendships. The loyalty of Ruth serves as a timeless reminder for you today. Ruth's devotion to Naomi goes beyond societal norms and expectations of that era, demonstrating that true friendships transcend cultural barriers, personal losses, and even life-altering decisions. The Book of Ruth in the Bible is a testament to the power of loyalty, love, and faith between two women.

Your True Self

The pressure is everywhere—to fit in, be liked, and keep up with trends. Social media doesn't help either, with constant comparisons and "friendship goals." This can lead to feelings of inadequacy. Much like Ruth and Naomi sought authenticity in their relationship, it's vital to seek genuine connections. Recognizing that friendships need to embrace this authentic self, instead of a version influenced by external pressures, can be liberating.

Just Patricia and Maria

High school began at Jericho. Patricia met Maria. On their first day, Patricia, with her quiet demeanor, and Maria, all smiles and words, sat side by side in English. Their unlikely friendship had traces of Naomi and Ruth's bond, different yet connected at the core. It was odd, like oil and water. Yet, with its funny way of mixing things, the universe made them friends.

They'd share sandwiches and secrets. Maria always talking, always moving. Patricia? She listened. She noticed everything—like how Maria's laugh changed when certain people were around. Or how she started wearing brighter lipsticks as the year went by.

Maria became popular. Patricia saw it coming before Maria did. The school was big, but Maria's name was everywhere. Maria's popularity skyrocketed, and Patricia felt left behind. Lunches without Maria became frequent for Patricia. Whispers, glances—they all told Patricia one thing: Maria's world was changing. And maybe, Patricia wasn't in it.

Then, the project happened. The universe's sense of humor, maybe. The teacher paired the two of them. Patricia felt the tension the first day they sat together, project papers between them. Patricia scribbled notes; Maria was distracted. Her phone kept buzzing. Each vibration took away a bit of Maria, Patricia thought.

It was when the fourth call in an hour came, Maria snapped. She turned the phone face down, tears welling up. "Everyone wants a piece of me, but no one really knows me," she whispered. Maria confided in Patricia, sharing her struggles with her newfound popularity and the constant need to fit in.

Patricia, taken aback, realized she wasn't the only one feeling adrift. Here was Maria, the heart of every party, equally lost. Patricia didn't say anything. She just passed a tissue. She understood, though. Watching Maria, she always understood more than Maria thought she did.

The room was silent for a long time. Just the hum of the air conditioner and Maria's quiet sniffling. "Remember our first lunch?" Maria broke the silence. Patricia nodded. "I miss that. Just...us. No noise."

The project nights became their haven. They worked, sure. But more than that, they found their rhythm again. Laughs, quiet conversations, and sometimes just silence. They finished the project, but something more important was rebuilt: trust.

The school year ended. Maria, still in the limelight, but now with Patricia by her side. Not behind or ahead, but beside. People noticed, or maybe they didn't. It didn't matter to Patricia. Because in the noise of high school, in the chaos of growing up, Patricia and Maria had found their quiet corner. And that was enough.

Daily Dose of Faith

* Start your day with a prayer, asking God to bless your friendships, to infuse them with understanding, patience, and love.

* Reflect on Proverbs 27:9, "Ointment and perfume rejoice the heart: so doth the sweetness of a man's friend by hearty counsel."

Living the Faith

Here's another example to consider. Mei always prays before making decisions. Like Ruth seeking God's guidance when choosing to stay with Naomi, when a rift occurs in her friend circle due to a misunderstanding, she prays for clarity and guidance instead of immediately taking sides.

This helps her approach the situation calmly, allowing for a resolution grounded in understanding and forgiveness.

Journal Time!

* Have you ever had someone who stood by you against all odds? Just as Ruth stood by Naomi, write about this experience.

* Are there moments you've felt pressured to change for a friend? Reflect on how it made you feel and how you can address it in the future.

* Think about your closest friendships. What values anchor these relationships?

Wrapping Up the Week

As you journey through the challenges and joys of friendships, ground them in faith and lessons from the past, and let them be bonds that illuminate your path. These relationships play a vital role in shaping who you become. Grounding them in God's teachings ensures they're not just temporary bonds but lifetime connections. So, as you navigate the maze of friendships, let faith be your guiding star.

Week 4: Cultivate a Strong Prayer Life

"Do not be anxious about anything, but in every situation, by prayer and petition, with thanksgiving, present your requests to God. And the peace of God, which transcends all understanding, will guard your hearts and your minds in Christ Jesus."

—Philippians 4:6-7

Recommended Readings:
Psalms 42, 62, 143

Alright! This week is about leveling up your relationship with God through prayer. Much like how Jesus consistently turned to prayer during his time on earth, think of it as sending a DM to the creator of the universe, where He's always online and never leaves you on "read."

Dive into Jesus's times. His life reminds you of prayer's undeniable importance in facing life's challenges. He was the busiest guy around—healing, teaching, dealing with drama. Yet, He took time to chill and pray. Luke 11 is kinda like Jesus giving you the ultimate DM template (a.k.a. the Lord's Prayer). It covers praising God, asking for help, and seeking guidance. The Psalms are like ancient songs of the heart—raw, real, and relatable, showing you that it's okay to be vulnerable with God.

Your True Self

In moments of doubt or fear, remember that turning to prayer, as Jesus did, can provide solace. Life is a wild ride. Insta-perfect lives can make your real-life struggles feel isolating. But guess what? You're not alone. God wants to hear every thought, fear, and emoji-heart-filled joy in your life. Through prayer, you can find authentic connections in a world of filters.

In the Calm and the Chaos

Michelle's room was a refuge from chaos outside. But even in the most peaceful environments, life can test your faith, pushing you toward prayer. Michelle's phone buzzed with a barrage of notifications— messages about the school project due next week, group chats filled with the latest friendship fallout, and one singular message from her mom: "Grandma's taken a turn for the worse."

The walls seemed to inch closer. She felt overwhelmed, like she was standing at the edge of a precipice. And in that quiet, desperate moment, with tears threatening to spill, she whispered, "Help, God! I can't do this." The plea was raw, like a wounded animal calling out.

Michelle didn't know she needed God—or what she expected now. But in the stillness that followed, she felt an inexplicable warmth.

Beginning that day, Michelle formed a habit. Before bed, she would sit by her window every night, looking out at the crescent moon, and talk to God. Sometimes it was a casual chat, other times, a fervent prayer. But every night, without fail, she reached out. She'd never been religious, never been one to pray. Yet, now, speaking to God felt like talking to an old friend—one who listened, without judgment, without any need for a response.

Sometimes, she doubted herself, wondering if she was just talking into the void. Like the day of her math exam, when anxiety gripped her, she whispered a quick prayer and felt a sudden surge of confidence. Or the night she learned her grandma had been moved to intensive care. Michelle sobbed, her voice hoarse, whispering her hopes and fears into the dark. She continued to pray. For Michelle, prayer was about comfort, the idea that someone out there was listening, providing strength when she felt she had none left.

When friendship dramas erupted at school, Michelle learned to step back, take a deep breath, and send a silent prayer. It gave her perspective, the ability to navigate teenage turbulence with a grace she never knew she possessed.

Grandma's illness was a long, drawn-out affair. Nights at the hospital, watching the frail figure in the bed, became a routine. Michelle's whispered conversations with God continued through it all, her anchor in the stormy seas. The chaos of life didn't dissipate. But in Michelle's heart, a quiet strength had taken root. And with it, she realized she could face any storm that came her way.

One evening, as she sat beside her grandma's bed, her grandmother, now recovering, whispered, "You have strength in you, Michelle. I've seen it these past weeks. Remember to always lean on it."

Michelle smiled, squeezing her grandma's hand. The strength her grandma spoke of wasn't just her own; it was the culmination of every whispered prayer, every plea, every hope she had shared with God.

Daily Dose of Faith

The same way Jesus made time to connect with God, you too can integrate prayer into your daily routine. Try the "Three-Times-Chime." Set three alarms on your phone daily. One for morning, noon, and night. When it chimes, take a minute, just sixty seconds, to shoot a prayer upwards. Maybe it's gratitude, a request, or a shoutout for a friend. Watch how this simple act transforms your day!

Living the Faith

Just as Jesus lived out the words he prayed, let your actions reflect your conversations with God. Ever heard the saying, "Walk it like you talk it"? Well, that's how you should be with your faith. If you're praying for patience and courage, look out for daily opportunities to put that into action. Maybe it's taking a deep breath when you're about to snap at a sibling, speaking up when you see someone being treated unfairly, showing kindness to a stranger, or standing up against bullying. Let your prayers guide your actions.

Journal Time!

* Reflecting on Jesus's prayer life can inspire your own. Pop quiz! How often do you pray? No judgment, just an honest check-in.

* Draft a tweet-length prayer. Short, impactful, and straight from the heart. Go!

* Think about a friend who could use some love. How can you include them in your prayers this week?

Wrapping Up the Week

Jesus's consistent communication with God is a guiding light for you. You can always pray in moments of joy, sorrow, doubt, or gratitude. It's your bridge to unwavering love, guidance, and strength. Here's the deal: life's going to throw curveballs. Prayer isn't about dodging them but finding the strength to hit them out of the park. You've got direct access to the ultimate source of power, comfort, and guidance. So, slide into God's DMs and keep that conversation going!

Week 5: Discover Your Spiritual Gifts

"Each of you should use whatever gift you have received to serve others, as faithful stewards of God's grace in its various forms."

—1 Peter 4:10

Recommended Reading:
The story of Mary Magdalene (John 20:11–18)

Ever felt like God has blessed you with a hidden superpower unique just to you? That's your spiritual gift waiting to be discovered! God's bestowed upon you special talents that aren't just for show. They're meant to shine, make a difference, and light up the world. This week, you're on a mission to uncover that power.

Drawing inspiration from the Bible can often illuminate our paths. Mary Magdalene is an emblem of faith and devotion in the New Testament. From being one of the women who supported Jesus and his disciples to being the first witness of His resurrection, Mary's spiritual journey is profound and transformative. Her gift was her steadfast devotion and clarity of vision.

Just as Mary stood firm in her faith and became a torchbearer of hope, you too have challenges to face and truths to proclaim. And just like Mary, you are equipped with gifts to make a difference. It wasn't about her status or past; it was her undeniable faith and unique perspective that allowed Mary to shine. Like Mary Magdalene, your gifts can bring light to the darkest moments, no matter how hidden or overlooked.

Your True Self

It's sometimes hard to hear your own voice while navigating high school, social media, and peer pressure. However, beyond those dramas, there's a voice inside you, guiding you toward your true purpose. Mary Magdalene found her voice through the uncertainties and challenges of her life; you too can discover yours despite the noise of everyday life. When you connect with that voice and find the special gift God's given you, life becomes an exciting journey of meaningful experiences.

Just as Mary had a unique spiritual gift of discernment and unwavering faith, you too have special gifts from God waiting to be recognized and harnessed. Reflect on your own connection with God. How might He reveal your spiritual gifts to you, even in unexpected moments? Dive deep into prayer, and ask God to illuminate those gifts within you, just as He did for Mary Magdalene. Your gifts have a purpose in God's grand design, and, like Mary, you are called to use them for His glory.

Angela's Awakening

Just as Mary Magdalene was an unexpected disciple among the many followers of Jesus, Angela felt like another face in the crowd. Angela always felt like she was floating. Whether at school or church, she often found herself lost in the sea of faces, unsure of where she fit in. She was quiet, observant, and most of the time, felt painfully ordinary.

Angela stumbled upon an unexpected opportunity during the summer of her sixteenth year. A family friend mentioned an internship at the local community center. Having no concrete plans, Angela decided to take a chance on it. It wasn't a glamorous gig. Initially, she did menial tasks: setting up meeting rooms, preparing refreshment stands, and handing out pamphlets. But as the weeks went by, something changed.

It began with a children's painting event. The assigned coordinator fell ill, and Angela was thrust into the organizer role.

She hesitated, her self-doubt creeping in. But with gentle nudging from her mentor, Mrs. Collins, she took charge.

It was like watching a flower bloom. Angela tapped into an unknown reservoir of confidence and clarity. She arranged the supplies, delegated responsibilities, handled a minor crisis when they ran out of blue paint, and encouraged the shy kids to express themselves. She sat late into the evenings, pouring over plans and details, ensuring everyone's needs were met. Mrs. Collins often found her absorbed in her work and smiled, seeing the spark in Angela that had been dormant for so long.

After the painting event's success, Angela's responsibilities at the center grew. From a simple art activity, she moved on to coordinating a local charity run, then a summer fair, and even a musical night. She began bringing teams together, coordinating events with the confidence of a star quarterback leading their team. The community, young and old, began to look forward to what Angela would come up with next. Her events were crafted with heart and care.

One afternoon, as they sat together over tea, Mrs. Collins remarked, "Angela, everyone has a gift. Mary Magdalene had her devotion; you have your leadership. It just takes the right moment for us to realize it."

Angela looked up, her eyes shimmering with newfound realization. "Leadership," she whispered. "That's my gift." She nodded. "It's been there all along, just waiting for the right moment to shine."

The summer ended, but Angela's journey had just begun. Back at church, the quiet girl in the background was now the vibrant young woman taking the initiative, leading groups, and sharing her newfound passion. She realized that, like her, others were also waiting to discover their spiritual gift.

Angela started a group in her church to help others find and embrace their unique gifts. Whether it was singing, teaching, counseling, or countless other roles, Angela made it her mission to help everyone realize their potential.

34

It's easy to feel lost in a crowd, to think you might not have a special skill or gift. But as Angela's story shows, sometimes all it takes is one summer, one opportunity, to awaken the leader within. Everyone has a gift waiting to be discovered; it's just a matter of finding the right moment to let it shine.

Daily Dose of Faith

Just as Mary Magdalene embraced her role as a devoted follower, step up and embrace your spiritual gifts this week. Ready for a challenge? You could dive into a hobby you've always been curious about, volunteer in a new role at your church, or even just help a neighbor or friend in a unique way. Every step you take could lead you closer to your spiritual gift.

Living the Faith

Mary's unwavering devotion was her spiritual gift, guiding her as one of Jesus's closest followers. The Gospel of John (John 20:11–18) gives us a touching account of Mary Magdalene's encounter with the risen Jesus. After discovering the empty tomb, Mary was in deep grief. But in her most despairing moment, she was blessed with the spiritual gift of discernment. She recognized Jesus when others didn't. Her deep connection and love for Christ allowed her to see Him, even when His appearance was changed.

Think of your spiritual gift as your personal brand of magic. Just like Angela, when you tap into it and serve others, you spread love and joy, and deepen your connection with God.

Journal Time!

* If you were a superhero, what would be your power? Why?
* Recall a time when you felt truly alive and happy. What were you doing?

* Think about your closest friends. If you had to identify one spiritual gift for each of them, what would it be?

Wrapping Up the Week

As you journey forward, remember the tales of Mary Magdalene and Angela. Discovering your spiritual gift isn't just a one-time revelation; it's an ongoing adventure. Your connection with God and understanding of your gifts will deepen as you evolve and grow. Keep searching, keep shining, and embrace the unique magic you bring to the world!

Week 6: Overcome Fear and Anxiety

"So do not fear, for I am with you; do not be dismayed, for I am your God. I will strengthen you and help you; I will uphold you with my righteous right hand."

—Isaiah 41:10

Recommended Reading:
The story of Elijah's victory over the prophets of Baal
(1 Kings 18)

From school assignments to friendship dramas, and even social media likes, there are a thousand things that might be causing you fear and anxiety. Just as Elijah stood firm against overwhelming odds, you can confidently face your challenges. Here's some good news: you're not alone in this, and with a sprinkle of faith, a dash of courage, and God's enduring love, you can face and overcome these feelings.

In 1 Kings 18, the prophet Elijah stood alone against 450 prophets of Baal. Even though he was outnumbered, his faith in God never wavered. He challenged the prophets to a contest to prove whose God was real. Despite the odds and possible fears, Elijah triumphed as God answered his prayer by sending fire from the heavens. In your life too, your challenges, no matter how overwhelming, can be overcome when you place your faith in God. Like Elijah, even when you feel outnumbered by your fears, God is with you, ensuring you're never truly alone.

Your True Self

The world today is a whirlwind of demands. With the pressures of grades, social expectations, and digital personas, it's easy to feel overwhelmed. But remember, your true worth isn't measured by these transient standards but by God's enduring love.

A Dance Beyond Fear

The chatter in the hallways was almost always about one thing: the upcoming prom. Jessica, a bubbly junior with a penchant for dreaming big, had doodled countless dresses in the margins of her notebooks. She imagined herself gliding across the dance floor, laughing with friends, capturing those cinematic moments of high school she had seen in countless movies.

But as the days ticked closer to that magical evening, a cloud began to cast a shadow over Jessica's excitement. Every time she thought about the prom, her heart raced—but not with joy. She imagined the whispers behind hands, the glances exchanged at her dress or shoes, and the unflattering photos that might circulate the next day. These fears turned her enthusiasm into anxiety.

One evening, in the sanctuary of the church's youth group meeting, Jessica mustered the courage to voice her fears. To her surprise, she wasn't alone. Mark was worried about his height and being shorter than his date. Lila was anxious about dancing in public. Emily feared she'd stand out too much because she was opting for a pantsuit instead of a traditional dress. Their individual fears wove together a complex pattern of insecurities.

And it was Rachel, the quietest of them all, who proposed an idea: "What if we turn our fears into strengths? Instead of focusing on what could go wrong, why don't we support one another, reminding each other of our value in God's eyes?"

It was a simple plan, but it resonated with everyone. They created a pact. Leading up to the prom, they would meet for small pep talks, share scriptures that uplifted them, and pray together. They started a group chat where any member could share a worry and receive a wave of reassurance.

Jessica's mom noticed the change in her daughter. Instead of fretting over which dress to buy, Jessica focused on finding something she genuinely loved, regardless of what was trendy. When Emily was unsure about her pantsuit, Jessica and the others rallied around her, telling her how confident and unique she looked.

On prom night, the group met beforehand. They weren't the most popular or glamorous group, but they radiated genuine happiness. They prayed together, asking God to guide them through the evening, to let them find joy in the simple moments, and to remember their worth wasn't in the opinions of others but in His unwavering love.

The night wasn't without its hitches. There were a few missteps on the dance floor and occasional awkward moments. But whenever one felt out of place, another would offer a reassuring smile or a comforting hand.

As the night came to a close, Jessica and her friends stood outside, their shoes in hand, laughing about the night's unexpected turns. The prom wasn't perfect, but it was theirs, a night where they danced with their feet and with their souls, held aloft by faith and friendship.

In the end, it wasn't just about a dance. It was a testament to the strength found in unity and the power of faith to transform fear into joy.

Daily Dose of Faith

When fear strikes, take a deep breath and draw strength from stories of faith like Elijah's. Reflect on verses like Isaiah 41:10, reminding yourself, "With God, I am fearless."

Living the Faith

Here's another example to consider. Beatrice's nervousness about public speaking is something many can relate to. When chosen to lead a class presentation, she tackled her fear head-on. By relying on her faith, she found strength she never knew she had.

Journal Time!

* Think about a recent time you felt anxious or fearful. How did it feel physically and emotionally?
* Remember a situation where you overcame a fear. What did you learn about yourself? How did God play a role in this?
* Challenge: This week, reflect on a fear or anxiety you face often. Drawing inspiration from the stories shared, what steps can you take to address this fear? Write about your plan and intentions.

Wrapping Up the Week

Life will always have its share of ups and downs. Fear and anxiety will come, but they don't define you. Like Elijah, with his unyielding faith against overwhelming odds, with faith, a loving community, and God's eternal presence, you can overcome anything. Embrace the journey, trust in God, and watch as your fears turn into tales of triumph. Life will always present challenges. But with faith, community, and God's presence, you're equipped to overcome them. As you move into the next week, what's one step you'll take to face fear with faith?

Week 7: Embrace the Power of Forgiveness

"Be kind and compassionate to one another, forgiving each other, just as in Christ God forgave you."
—Ephesians 4:32

Recommended Reading:
The story of Jesus being anointed by a sinful woman
(Luke 7:36–50)

We all have moments of regret, mistakes, or trespasses against others. Embracing forgiveness can often seem more challenging than holding onto resentment. However, as the story in Luke 7 demonstrates, when we come before God with genuine repentance, He grants us profound mercy. This week, tap into the boundless strength of forgiveness.

In Luke 7:36–50, during a dinner at a Pharisee's house, a sinful woman entered with an alabaster jar of expensive perfume. She stood behind Jesus, weeping, and wet His feet with her tears. She wiped them with her hair, kissed them, and poured perfume on them. The Pharisee, named Simon, thought to himself that if Jesus were truly a prophet, He would know who this woman was and what kind of life she led. Jesus, knowing Simon's thoughts, told him a parable about two debtors, emphasizing the greater love shown by the one who had been forgiven more.
He then turned to the woman and said, "Your sins are forgiven."
This account highlights the depth of Jesus's mercy and underscores the rejuvenating and redeeming power of forgiveness.

Your True Self

In the ever-evolving world of drama—be it from school, friends, or even online—it's so easy to get caught up in the hurt. However, when you reflect upon the sinful woman from Luke 7, who approached Jesus with genuine repentance and was graciously forgiven, you recognize the transformative power of mercy. Sometimes you feel wronged, and the idea of holding a grudge seems all too tempting. But remember this: harboring resentment can overshadow the radiant soul you truly are. The essence of your true self flourishes in love, understanding, and forgiveness.

The Silent Months

Marisol and Taylor were best friends; everyone at Covenant Middle School knew it. From shared secret handshakes to their love for vintage comics, they had been inseparable since the fifth grade. The duo faced every challenge and every awkward moment and celebrated every triumph together. So, when a misunderstood text threw a wrench into their seemingly unbreakable bond, the entire school was shocked.

It began innocently enough. Marisol sent a text one evening, a simple one: "I saw him with someone else today." It was meant to refer to their shared crush on a TV character they both adored, but the missing context made Taylor read it as real-life gossip about her recent ex-boyfriend. Words were taken out of context, leading to feelings of hurt and betrayal. Neither wanted to be the first to admit they might have overreacted. Fueled by hurt and pride, a slight misunderstanding became a chasm between them. Each day that passed without resolution added layers to their initial pain.

Weeks turned into months. They sat on opposite sides of the classroom and avoided eye contact in the hallways. Their mutual friends found themselves in the unfortunate position of having to pick sides. The absence of their usual laughter and inside jokes created an echoing void in the lives of everyone who knew them.

One crisp Sunday morning, Marisol found herself in church, the weight of the strained friendship heavy on her mind. As the pastor began his sermon on forgiveness, she felt each word resonate within her, as if they were being spoken directly to her. The pastor spoke of the strength in letting go, the healing power of forgiveness, and the importance of mending broken ties. After the service, clutching the church bulletin as if it were a lifeline, Marisol made a decision. She took out her phone, her fingers hovering hesitantly over the keyboard, and typed out a message to Taylor: "Can we meet? I miss us."

The two met at their favorite spot, a quiet corner in the local park where they'd spent countless hours talking and dreaming. They sat far apart on the bench, separated by a heavy silence. But Marisol took a deep breath, bridged the gap, and began with a simple, "I'm sorry."

Taylor looked up, her eyes brimming with tears, "I've missed us too."

They spoke for hours, dissecting the miscommunication, addressing the hurt, and reminiscing about the good times. There was laughter, there were tears, and most importantly, there was healing.

Marisol realized it wasn't just about apologizing. It was about taking responsibility, understanding each other's perspective, and valuing their bond over pride. Taylor recognized the importance of communication and how easy it was to let minor misunderstandings escalate.

Their reunion was not just a rekindling of old ties but a forging of new ones—stronger, more understanding, and deeply empathetic. They learned that friendships, like all relationships, require work, understanding, and, sometimes, a leap of faith. The rift that once seemed insurmountable became a testament to their bond, proving that any hurdle can be overcome with effort, understanding, and a touch of grace.

Daily Dose of Faith

Consider starting your mornings with a simple affirmation: "Today, I choose love over anger, understanding over judgment, and forgiveness over resentment." Remember the mercy Jesus showed in Luke 7. Hold onto this intention throughout your day, and when faced with challenges, let these words guide your heart.

Living the Faith

Here's another example to consider. Sophie always felt overshadowed by her younger sister, Marie-Christine, who seemed to excel in everything. One day, Sophie discovered Marie-Christine had borrowed her favorite dress without asking. In anger, Sophie tore up Marie-Christine's art project. When she realized the depth of her actions, Sophie turned to prayer. She sought God's guidance in mending their relationship. After a heartfelt conversation, the sisters forgave each other and began appreciating and supporting one another's talents. Their reconciliation, inspired by divine teachings of forgiveness, showed the same kind of mercy that Jesus exemplified.

Journal Time!

* We all have moments of struggle and understanding. Reflect on a time when you found it hard to forgive someone. How did that situation affect your emotions and overall well-being?

* Imagine a scenario where you forgive that person. How does that make you feel? Lighter? Freer?

* Think about a time when you sought forgiveness. How did others' understanding (or lack thereof) influence your feelings and actions?

* Write a letter (you don't have to send it) to someone you want to forgive. Pour out your feelings and end with words of forgiveness.

Wrapping Up the Week

Forgiveness is a profound act that can change lives, heal deep wounds, mend relationships, and usher in a newfound sense of peace. While forgiving might not change the past, it can change the future. Through God's love and guidance, choose to be an exemplar of forgiveness and love in this world.

Week 8: Develop a Servant's Heart

"For even the Son of Man did not come to be served, but to serve, and to give his life as a ransom for many."
—Mark 10:45

Recommended Reading:
The story of the woman at the well (John 4:1–26)

There's unparalleled beauty in extending a helping hand and opening your heart to those around you. This week, you'll embark on a beautiful journey of cultivating a servant's heart, enriching your life and those you touch. Just as Jesus reached out to the Samaritan woman in John 4:1–26, you are encouraged to extend your hand to those around you.

Jesus, tired from his journey, sat by a well in Samaria. A Samaritan woman came to draw water, and Jesus asked her for a drink. Surprised, as Jews didn't associate with Samaritans, she questioned Him. Jesus spoke of the "living water," which led to a deeper conversation about faith, worship, and truth. Jesus, through His act of service and genuine conversation, transformed her life. The woman, filled with newfound belief, became an ambassador of Christ's love, sharing her experience with many.

Your True Self

With the whirlwind of school, social media, and trying to fit in, it's easy to become self-focused. Yet, deep down, your soul craves genuine connections and actions that make a difference. Much like how Jesus took the time to connect deeply with the Samaritan woman, your true self thrives not in the number of likes you get but in the number of lives you touch.

The Empty Chair

The cafeteria was a buzz of excitement each day, filled with the familiar sounds of clinking trays, laughter, and the constant hum of chatter. In this dynamic atmosphere, there was always an anomaly: Lucy, who sat by herself at the end of a table, her tray containing little more than a sandwich and a bottle of water. Her eyes would often be fixed on a book or staring blankly at some distant point.

Fabienne, a lively junior with a wide group of friends, couldn't help but notice. Day after day, while she laughed and chatted with her group, her eyes would drift toward Lucy. In such moments, she was reminded of the lessons from Jesus's interaction at the well. Driven by a spirit akin to Christ's own, a spirit of service and compassion, Fabienne decided to break her routine. She picked up her tray, took a deep breath, and headed toward Lucy's table.

"Is this seat taken?" Fabienne asked, pointing to the empty space next to Lucy.

Lucy, caught off guard, simply shook her head. "It's open."

The first few minutes were filled with awkward silences and hesitant glances. Fabienne tried to keep the conversation light, asking about Lucy's classes and her favorite subjects. Slowly, Lucy began to open up.

"I moved here a couple of months ago," she started, playing with the crust of her sandwich. "It's been...different."

Fabienne nodded, urging her on. Over the next few weeks, the two met regularly during lunch. The conversations flowed more freely each day, and Lucy's walls began to come down. "Today would've been my mom's birthday," she admitted one day, voice quivering slightly, her eyes more tired than usual. "She passed away last year."

Fabienne felt a pang in her chest, realizing the weight Lucy had been carrying alone. She reached across the table, covering Lucy's hand with her own. No words were spoken, but the gesture spoke of understanding and compassion.

As spring turned to summer, Lucy and Fabienne's bond grew stronger. They found solace in shared stories, laughter, and comfortable silences. The school began to see a transformation in Lucy. From a reserved newcomer, she blossomed into an active community member, joining clubs and even helping Fabienne organize a support group for students dealing with grief.

For Fabienne, the experience was transformative. Guided by a spirit of service reminiscent of Jesus's approach, she had reached out and found a lifelong friend. The power of a simple act of kindness, she realized, could ripple through lives in ways she hadn't imagined.

On the last day of school, Fabienne and Lucy sat side by side, surrounded by a group of friends, laughter echoing around them. They shared glances, a silent acknowledgment of the journey they'd taken together.

In that bustling cafeteria, no chairs remained empty.

Daily Dose of Faith

Make it a mission to perform at least one act of kindness daily. Remember the Samaritan woman and how a simple act of service from Jesus changed her life. It could be as simple as complimenting someone, assisting a teacher after class, or listening to a friend. These little acts nourish your soul and ripple out into the world in ways you might not even see.

Living the Faith

Here's another example to consider. Every Saturday, Ailani tutored younger students in her community who struggled academically. This act of service, inspired by the kindness Jesus displayed to the Samaritan woman, not only boosted their confidence but also filled Ailani with a sense of purpose.

Journal Time!

* Think of someone in your life or community who could use help or companionship. What small act of service can you offer them?

* Reflect on a time when someone served or helped you selflessly. How did that make you feel?

* Jesus took the time to truly listen and converse with the Samaritan woman. Who in your life can you offer the gift of genuine listening?

* Journal about a community or school project you'd like to start or join that embodies the spirit of serving others.

Wrapping Up the Week

Drawing inspiration from Jesus's kindness toward the Samaritan woman, you can see the value of service. In a world that often prioritizes self-promotion, choosing to serve becomes a revolutionary act. Through service, you uplift others and discover a deeper sense of purpose and connection. As you walk this path, remember, developing a servant's heart isn't about grand gestures but heartfelt moments of kindness and love. Be the change, one act of service at a time.

Week 9: Honor Your Parents and Guardians

"Honor your father and your mother, so that you may live long in the land the Lord your God is giving you."
—Exodus 20:12

Recommended Reading:
The story of Joseph and his father, Jacob (Genesis 37–50)

This week, you'll dive into the heart of your home, exploring the relationship with your parents and guardians. While they might not always understand your latest trends or choices, they offer invaluable wisdom and love. Much like Joseph and his father, Jacob, whose relationship transcended adversity, misunderstandings, and distance, you are reminded of the bond you share with your parents.

The bond between Joseph and Jacob is a profound testament to the love between a parent and child. Jacob cherished Joseph, evident from the special coat he gave him. This favoritism, however, led to envy among Joseph's brothers, culminating in them selling Joseph into slavery. Despite the challenges and distance, the bond between Joseph and Jacob remained unwavering. Their eventual reunion in Egypt is one of the Bible's most touching moments, underscoring the enduring connection between parents and their children.

Your True Self

In the ocean of peer pressure, school stresses, and the dizzying speed of growing up, your parents or guardians act as anchors. They might not have had your social media, but they faced their own troubles. Jacob's deep love for Joseph was symbolized by a unique coat he gifted him, signifying his special place in the family. Similarly, your parents often express their affection and concerns in their own unique ways. Honoring them doesn't mean always agreeing, but understanding that at the heart of most of their decisions is love for you.

Echoes from the Past

Samantha and her mother always shared a close bond—one forged over whispered secrets, shared laughter, and countless shopping trips. But soon, the dynamic began to shift. Samantha's growing desire for independence sometimes clashed with her mother's protective instincts.

The cozy kitchen, which used to resonate with the warmth of cookie-baking sessions and jovial chats, had become an arena for arguments. "Why can't I stay out until midnight? Everyone else does!" Samantha would exclaim. Her mother's reply, filled with concern, was always, "It's not safe, and you have school." Samantha's grades, once stellar, were slipping, and her new friends, in her mother's eyes, were a wild bunch. Conversations that used to flow effortlessly now felt like navigating a minefield.

One chilly Saturday afternoon, after a particularly intense disagreement about a sleepover, Samantha stomped to her room. She just wanted to escape, to drown out her frustrations. As she rifled through a drawer for her headphones, an old, yellowed envelope slipped out from between its pages. The handwriting was distinctly her mother's, but younger, more free-flowing. The recipient? Grandma June.

Drawn by curiosity and the need for distraction, Samantha unfolded the letter.

"Dear Mom," it began, "I can't believe you won't let me go to Stacey's party! You say you're worried about me, but all you're doing is ruining my life!"

As Samantha read on, a sense of déjà vu washed over her. The letter was eerily similar to her countless arguments with her mother. It talked of feeling confined, of friends her grandma disapproved of, and slipping grades. But what struck Samantha most was the closing: "...but despite all this, I know deep down you do this because you love me. I may not understand it now, but I hope one day I will."

Samantha sat back, the letter's weight far heavier than its frail pages suggested. Here, in her hands, was proof that the battles she fought with her mother were not unique to them. Her mother, too, had gone through the same struggles with her grandmother.

She hesitated for a moment, then knocked softly on her mother's door. Without waiting, she stepped inside, finding her mom seated on the bed, looking worn out. The two locked eyes, words unnecessary. Samantha held up the letter, her mother's eyes widening in recognition.

Before words were spoken, they hugged. A long, tight hug, communicating more than words ever could. Samantha felt her frustrations melt away, replaced by understanding. They might still have disagreements, but beneath it all, she knew her mother's motivations were rooted in love.

The letter found its place in Samantha's diary. A reminder that growing pains were just a phase, and much like the undying love Jacob had for Joseph, even through separation and hardships, love between a parent and child was forever.

Daily Dose of Faith

Make it a point to spend quality time with your parents or guardians. It could be a simple coffee chat, cooking together, or sharing stories from your day. These moments can bridge gaps and nurture understanding.

Living the Faith

Here's another example to consider. Rebecca started a tradition: she and her dad would watch old classic movies together every Sunday evening. Initially, it was a way to escape her chores, but it soon became their bonding ritual. Through these movies, they shared laughs, discussed life lessons, and Rebecca saw a side of her dad she'd never known—his teenage self.

Journal Time!

* Write about a cherished memory you have with your parents or guardians.

* Reflect on a time when you disagreed with them. Now, try to view the situation from their perspective. What new insights do you gain?

* If there's a barrier or misunderstanding between you and a parent/guardian, journal about potential steps you can take to bridge that gap.

* Write a letter to a parent or guardian, expressing your feelings, gratitude, and love. You can choose to share it with them or keep it for yourself.

Wrapping Up the Week

Navigating everyday life with your parents or guardians can be challenging. Sometimes you're in harmony, and sometimes you face disagreements. Yet, with understanding, patience, and love, you can foster a bond that withstands the test of time. This week, honor the love, sacrifices, and lessons your parents and guardians have given you, cherishing the heartbeats that have echoed alongside yours since the beginning.

Week 10: Manage Stress and Time

"Do not be anxious about anything, but in every situation, by prayer and petition, with thanksgiving, present your requests to God. And the peace of God, which transcends all understanding, will guard your hearts and your minds in Christ Jesus."

—Philippians 4:6–7

> **Recommended Reading:**
> The story of Mary and Martha in Luke 10:38–42

In a world that moves relentlessly, it's easy to feel overwhelmed. But what if I told you that you could be productive without the stress? It's all about balance, prioritizing, and understanding that it's okay to take a breather. Dive in and navigate the art of managing stress and mastering time, much like Mary and Martha navigated their roles and responsibilities.

In the Gospel of Luke, you'll encounter Mary and Martha, two sisters whose contrasting choices about time and commitment teach you profound lessons about balance and inner peace. While Martha was busy with preparations, Mary chose to sit at Jesus's feet, listening to his teachings. When Martha voiced her frustration about handling tasks alone, Jesus said, "Martha, Martha, you are worried and upset about many things, but few things are needed—or indeed only one. Mary has chosen what is better, and it will not be taken away from her." This story reminds you to prioritize your spiritual well-being amidst daily tasks.

Your True Self

You're juggling school, hobbies, social life, and maybe even a part-time job. Much like Martha felt the weight of her responsibilities, you too might be stretched thin. In the whirlwind of achievements and expectations, it's essential to remember you are more than your accomplishments. Overloading can lead to burnout. Instead, embracing time management can allow you to achieve your goals while preserving your peace, reminding you to sometimes choose the "Mary approach" and just be present.

Learning to Breathe

Amy had earned her title. As the "Do-It-All Girl" at Jericho High, she was everywhere, all the time. In some ways, her life mirrored Martha's— always active, always doing. The energy and poise she demonstrated while leading the dance team were the same qualities she brought to the charity drives. And when exam season rolled around? Amy always seemed one step ahead of everyone. Yet, beneath that high-achieving exterior, a storm was brewing.

The library was hushed that Tuesday afternoon. Most students were outside, basking in the beginning of summer. But Amy was indoors, surrounded by a fortress of textbooks and notes. Amy's busyness echoed Martha's, feeling the pressure of numerous responsibilities. The upcoming exams, dance rehearsals, and the looming charity event weighed on her, each commitment like a brick on her shoulders.

Lisa, her closest friend since childhood, witnessed Amy's walls finally crumble. Among the quiet rustling of pages and the distant ticking of the library's ancient clock, Amy's suppressed sobs seemed deafening. Lisa rushed to her side, wrapping an arm around her trembling friend. "Talk to me," she urged gently.

Amy took a shaky breath, feeling the weight of everything crashing down. "It's just...all too much. I can't do it all."

Lisa nodded, understanding all too well. "You remember the story of Mary and Martha?" she asked, referring to a tale they'd heard at Sunday school. This story, though ancient, was a reflection of what many feel today.

Amy blinked through her tears. "Remind me?"

"Martha was always busy, always doing. Mary, on the other hand, took the time to sit and listen, to be present." Lisa paused, letting the words sink in. "Sometimes, we need to be Mary. To pause and breathe."

Amy gave a weak smile. "I've been a Martha for so long. I don't know how to switch."

Lisa, ever the planner, grinned. "That's where I come in. Tomorrow, we're doing something different."

The next morning, Lisa wanted to show Amy something new. A way to connect with oneself, to find calm in the chaos. Sitting cross-legged on Amy's bedroom floor, they began a meditation session. They focused on their breaths, on being present. Much like Mary, Amy was learning the power of stillness. The weight on Amy's chest seemed to lighten.

Post-meditation, Lisa spread out a planner. "Time management," she declared. They blocked times for study, dance, and charity work, interspersing them with short breaks.

Amy looked at the organized schedule, hope dawning. "I...I can do this."

Weeks passed. The changes were subtle at first. Though still active in her commitments, Amy now moved with an air of calm. Meditation became her daily anchor, and the planner was her roadmap.

And as the days flowed into weeks, the tale of Mary and Martha took root in her heart. She realized the importance of balance, of sometimes stepping back to listen, reflect, and breathe.

The school year concluded with Amy's dance recital. As she swayed and leaped, her movements had a newfound grace, a depth that wasn't there before. After the final note played, the applause was thunderous. But the loudest claps and the brightest smile came from Lisa, who cheered from the front row.

The "Do-It-All Girl" was still very much present. Only now, she was also the "Takes-a-Moment Girl," finding a balance between the Martha and Mary within her. And it made all the difference.

Daily Dose of Faith

Every morning, set aside ten minutes for a quiet reflection. Think of this as your "Mary moment," a pause in the chaos. During this time, prioritize your tasks for the day. What needs immediate attention? What can wait? Seek God's guidance in these moments, asking Him to guide your steps and grant clarity.

Living the Faith

Here's another example to consider. When Reese felt overwhelmed, she began using the Pomodoro Technique—twenty-five minutes of focused work followed by a five-minute break. Instead of scrolling through her phone during breaks, she read a Bible verse, stretched, or just breathed. This technique was her way of interweaving "Martha tasks" with "Mary pauses," balancing productivity with spiritual grounding.

Journal Time!

* List out tasks that often overwhelm you. How can you approach them differently? Reflect on how to incorporate more "Mary moments" amid the "Martha tasks."

* Reflect on moments when you've felt most at peace. What were you doing? How can you integrate such moments into your daily life?

* Think about the moments when you've needed help but hesitated to ask. How can recognizing those moments and seeking support make a difference?

* Set achievable goals for the week. Celebrate small wins as you progress.

Wrapping Up the Week

Life isn't about filling every second, but finding purpose in every moment. It's recognizing when to be a Martha and when to embrace Mary's stillness. As you wrap up this week, strive to find balance and savor moments of quiet reflection. With God guiding your days, you can navigate life's challenges with grace and poise.

Week 11: Build Healthy Relationships

"Do to others as you would have them do to you."
—Luke 6:31

> **Recommended Reading:**
> The story of Paul and Barnabas (Acts 9:26–27)

Relationships are at the center of your life, be it friendships, family, or romantic ties. But like a garden, they need nurturing. Dive in to discover the secrets of cultivating genuine, nurturing, and steadfast relationships.

The trust Barnabas showed in Paul, even when others doubted him, highlights the foundation of any strong relationship: unwavering belief and trust in one another. When Paul, formerly known as Saul, converted to Christianity, many doubted his transformation. But Barnabas believed in him and introduced him to the apostles, vouching for his genuine encounter with Jesus. This act of trust changed the course of Paul's ministry. Their story emphasizes the power of faith in relationships and how sincere belief in someone can unleash their potential.

Your True Self

In an age of social media, the number of "friends" may seem essential. But quantity doesn't equal quality. Just as Barnabas saw the genuine heart of Paul, you should aim to recognize and nurture the authenticity in your relationships. Authentic relationships are based on trust, understanding, and mutual respect. It's about being present, listening, and growing together.

Bridging the Gap

Lila and Zoe had always been two halves of a whole. From swapping lunchbox treats in the first grade to late-night whispered secrets during sleepovers, their bond had been unwavering. Their friends often joked they were twins separated at birth, due to their uncanny ability to finish each other's sentences. But as the dizzying whirlwind of high school set in, their once-intertwined paths began to diverge.

Zoe was entranced by the world of drama. She loved the adrenaline of opening nights, the magic of slipping into a character, and the camaraderie among her theater mates. The school's auditorium became her second home. Lila, on the other hand, found her voice and passion in the debate club. She was driven by the intellectual sparring, the fast-paced arguments, and the satisfaction of a well-made point. Once filled with shared experiences, their lunchtime conversations slowly became a series of monologues about their separate worlds.

Just as Paul faced challenges and doubts from his peers after his conversion, Lila and Zoe struggled to maintain their bond as their interests evolved. There would have been misunderstandings, doubts, and distance. But with Barnabas's unwavering support, Paul bridged the divide.

Weekends, which they used to binge-watch movies or explore their town, became occupied with rehearsals and debate prep. Phone calls grew shorter, and the gap widened.

One day, Lila overheard some of her debate teammates talking. "Lila and Zoe? They barely hang out anymore," one remarked. The truth of that statement stung. That evening, Lila called Zoe. They talked, really talked, for the first time in months. They voiced their worries, unintentional neglect, and fear of growing apart.

Just as Barnabas extended a hand of trust to Paul during his time of transformation, Lila and Zoe took a moment to reconnect and understand each other better.

By the end of that call, they had a plan.

Summer arrived with its golden promise of free time and sunny days. Instead of taking up internships or summer courses, Lila and Zoe dedicated this summer to each other. They named it the "Summer of Rediscovery."

The first week, Zoe invited Lila to a local theater workshop. Lila felt out of her depth, but Zoe held her hand, explaining terms and guiding her through warm-up exercises. Lila even got a small part in a play. While she was no Meryl Streep, the thrill of being on stage, of sharing Zoe's world, was exhilarating.

The following week, it was Lila's turn. She roped Zoe into a mock debate. They researched and prepared arguments, and Zoe got a taste of the high-paced world of debate. Initially hesitant, Zoe grew to appreciate the art of argumentation and even won a friendly debate against another team.

The summer was filled with theater rehearsals, debates, picnics, and heart-to-hearts. They walked in each other's shoes, gaining a newfound respect for their passions and rekindling their bond.

As senior year commenced, Lila and Zoe were once again inseparable. They had their individual commitments, but they also had a deeper understanding of each other. Their bond was a testament to the biblical principle of placing trust and understanding at the heart of relationships, much like Barnabas did with Paul. They realized that relationships, like plants, require nurturing and care. They need understanding, effort, and mutual respect to flourish.

One day, as they sat under their favorite tree, Zoe mused, "This summer taught me that it's not just about having common interests. It's about investing time to understand and appreciate our differences."

Lila smiled, squeezing her hand, "This summer reminded us of what truly matters: understanding, trust, and taking the time to nurture our bond. Just like Barnabas did for Paul."

Daily Dose of Faith

Practice active listening. When someone talks, truly listen without planning your response. This simple act can transform the depth of your conversations and relationships.

Living the Faith

Here's another example to consider. When Itzel noticed her friends drifting apart due to varied interests, she was inspired by the trust Barnabas placed in Paul. She organized a monthly "Share Day," encouraging everyone to understand and appreciate each other's passions, bridging the gaps in their friendships.

Journal Time!

* Think of a relationship that means a lot to you. What are its strengths? How can you make it even stronger?

* Reflect on a time when someone stood by you like Barnabas did for Paul. How did it feel?

* Are there relationships you've outgrown or that have become toxic? How can you address them with grace and kindness?

* Write a letter to a friend or family member, expressing gratitude, love, or an apology.

Wrapping Up the Week

Relationships aren't always easy, but they are worth every effort. Like Barnabas and Paul, your relationships can face challenges. Still, with understanding and faith, they can be strengthened. As you close this chapter, remember that building and maintaining healthy relationships is a journey of understanding, patience, and mutual respect. As you move forward, remember Barnabas's unwavering trust in Paul and strive to offer the same level of understanding and faith to the relationships in your own life.

Week 12: Find Your Purpose and Calling

"For we are God's handiwork, created in Christ Jesus to do good works, which God prepared in advance for us to do."

—Ephesians 2:10

Recommended Reading:
The story of Moses (Exodus 2:11–4:17)

You might find yourself chasing paths defined by society, parents, or peers. But there's a unique calling, a divine purpose for you. Like Moses, you too can discover your divine calling amidst your everyday life.

Moses, once a prince of Egypt, found himself in exile, tending to sheep. Yet, when God spoke to him through the burning bush, he was called for a greater purpose: to lead the Israelites out of slavery. Despite his doubts and fears, Moses embraced his divine mission, showcasing that your purpose often surpasses your immediate understanding and comfort zones.

Your True Self

In a world full of external influences, it's easy to lose your way, much like Moses before his encounter with the burning bush. But within every heart lies a special mission. It's the flame that ignites passion, the voice that whispers dreams, and the path that feels intrinsically right.

A Lesson in Purpose

Ava moved through life with a grace and success that stood out for her age. Captain of the school debate team, a gold medalist in the science fair, and first-chair violin in the school orchestra—her achievements read like a list too extensive for one person. But underneath the accolades and applause, an emptiness nagged at her. Similar to how Moses might have felt during his princely days in Egypt, the hollowness grew with every medal or certificate she added to her wall. Success, she felt, had become a checklist; there was no deeper meaning.

One day, her school announced a week-long community service trip to a rural school in a neighboring state. Thinking it might be a good resume booster, Ava signed up without giving it much thought. In this new environment, Ava, like Moses, would come to a turning point in understanding her true purpose. She packed her bags with stationery, books, and teaching aids, foreseeing a straightforward week of charity work.

Nothing prepared her for what she was about to experience.

Upon arrival, Ava was struck by the stark simplicity of the village. No fancy buildings, no technological marvels—just huts, farmlands, and the little school made of bricks and mortar. The school's playground was a simple clearing with a swing made of rope and a discarded tire.

As Ava entered a classroom, she was greeted by a sea of eager faces, eyes shining with anticipation. These kids had none of the privileges she took for granted, yet their thirst for knowledge was palpable. Every story she read, every problem she helped solve, and every question she answered was met with pure, unadulterated enthusiasm.

One afternoon, a little girl named Mira approached her. With a tattered notebook in hand, Mira asked Ava to help her with a math problem. Ava noticed the girl used a broken pencil, yet her notes were meticulous. As they worked through the problem, Mira's determination was evident. She wanted to learn, not for grades or praise, but for the sheer joy of understanding.

It was in that simple classroom, with chalk dust and sunlit benches, that Ava's perspective shifted. Accolades and achievements were valuable, yes. But the children's sincere desire to learn moved her more deeply. Their passion wasn't fueled by competition or societal expectations but by a genuine love for knowledge.

On the last day of the trip, the children put up a small farewell program for Ava and her classmates. Songs, dances, and heartfelt thank-you notes. As Ava boarded the bus to head home, Mira ran up to her, gifting her the broken pencil they had used. "For when you become a teacher," she whispered.

That simple pencil became Ava's most treasured possession. It was a reminder of the week that had redefined success for her. Teaching, she realized, was not just about imparting knowledge, but about igniting the spark of curiosity.

Ava returned home with a renewed sense of purpose. She began tutoring at local community centers and, soon after, pursued a degree in education. Her mission became clear—to be an educator who kindled flames of passion in young minds.

Years later, as Ava stood in her own classroom, she would often think back to that trip and the eager faces of the rural school. On her desk, among all the teaching tools, lay a reminder of her journey—a small, broken pencil. Just as Moses's staff symbolized his divine mission, the broken pencil became Ava's emblem of purpose.

Daily Dose of Faith

Set aside ten minutes daily to meditate or pray. Begin by finding a quiet space, taking a few deep breaths, and then focusing on the question, "What am I truly passionate about?" Contemplate how Moses might have felt when he first heard God's call and use that reflection as inspiration. Let the answers come naturally, without judgment.

Living the Faith

Here's another example to consider. Riley started a journal called "Passion Pages," where she'd jot down things that made her heart race. Drawing inspiration from Moses's journey, she decided to find her burning bush moment. Over time, patterns emerged, leading her to her calling as a wildlife conservationist.

Journal Time!

* List moments when you felt most alive or fulfilled. What were you doing? How can you integrate more of that into your life?

* Think about role models or mentors. What aspects of their lives or missions resonate with you?

* Without limitations, what would you want to achieve or become? Dream big.

* How does Moses's journey inspire you? In what ways do you relate to his initial reluctance and eventual acceptance of his calling?

Wrapping Up the Week

Your journey of self-discovery can be reminiscent of Moses: your true purpose can often be hidden in plain sight. As this week concludes, remain open to signs, and trust the unexpected turns, knowing your divine calling, like Moses's, may soon reveal itself.

Week 13: Balance School, Work, and Faith

"But seek first his kingdom and his righteousness, and all these things will be given to you as well."
—Matthew 6:33

Recommended Reading:
The story of Mary, Martha, and Lazarus (John 11:1–44)

In a world of hustle, striking a balance is challenging. But with faith as your compass, you can navigate through the chaos and find harmony.

In John 11, there's a captivating tale of Mary, Martha, and their brother Lazarus. Lazarus falls gravely ill, and the sisters find themselves submerged in the responsibilities of caring for their home and ailing brother. In their most desperate hour, they turn to Jesus. The subsequent miracle of raising Lazarus from the dead showcased Jesus's divine power. It highlighted the sisters' unwavering faith through the whirlwind of their responsibilities.

As Mary and Martha did with Lazarus, tending to a gravely ill family member requires immeasurable emotional, physical, and spiritual strength. Every day, the sisters would have been met with the draining tasks of ensuring Lazarus's comfort, administering remedies, praying for his recovery, and maintaining the household—all while grappling with the looming shadow of grief. Such challenges can easily make one lose sight of faith or hope. Yet, in their overwhelming responsibility and heartache, the sisters demonstrated a crucial lesson. By reaching out to Jesus in their time of suffering, they showed that faith doesn't wane in the face of adversity; instead, it becomes an essential lifeline. When faced with life's daunting challenges, it's this unwavering faith, intertwined with our daily duties, that guides us, providing hope and resilience.

Your True Self

From striving for academic excellence to securing financial stability, the pressures of today's world can often pull you in multiple directions. Amidst these demands, similar to Mary and Martha's balance between home responsibilities and faith, it's essential to remember that your spiritual well-being is paramount, and maintaining that balance fuels every other endeavor.

Snowfall and Second Chances

The day Serena stepped into Mocha Delights, the quaint café at the corner of Elm Street, she felt a rush. Her first paycheck, a sense of responsibility, and the joy of being a young barista were all exciting. But as days turned into weeks, the weight of juggling her senior year, shifts at the café, and her youth group sessions became palpable.

Serena's life, bustling with commitments, began to feel overwhelming. Just as Mary and Martha faced challenges, Serena felt the strain of balancing her priorities and faith. Her alarm clock buzzed unforgivingly at five thirty. After a hurried breakfast and sifting through notes for a quick study session, she'd rush to the café for her early shift. By evening, she'd head to youth group activities, her energy flagging but spirit resolute. "It's just a phase," she'd tell herself, but the reflection in the mirror told a different story—droopy eyes, tousled hair, and a perpetual yawn.

Her grades began to dip, and her once-enjoyable youth group sessions felt like a chore. Serena missed the laughter, the joy of diving into scriptures, and the camaraderie. Every night, as she fell into bed exhausted, a small voice within questioned if she was losing her essence in the whirlwind of activities.

Then came the snowstorm.

One chilly December morning, Serena woke up to the world painted in white. The town was blanketed in snow, making roads impassable. Everything came to a standstill. No school, no café shifts—it was an unexpected day off. Initially restless, Serena eventually curled up with a cup of hot cocoa, watching the snowflakes dance.

The stillness of the day was a stark contrast to her chaotic life. In this moment of pause, Serena, much like Mary and Martha, was reminded of the essence of faith. It provided a much-needed pause. Wrapped in a blanket with the soft glow of fairy lights, Serena began to reflect. She realized she had equated busyness with productivity, forgetting that rest wasn't just physical—it was spiritual. Her faith had taught her the importance of balance, of Sabbath—something she had neglected.

She took out her journal, a gift from her youth leader, and began to write. It started as a list but soon turned into a letter to God. She wrote about her exhaustion, her feelings of being adrift, and her longing to connect again. By the time she was done, her cocoa had gone cold, but her heart felt warmer.

Serena devised a plan. She spoke to her manager and rescheduled her shifts to allow for dedicated study time, ensuring she never missed her youth group meetings. She carved out moments in her day for prayer and reflection, even if it was just ten minutes before bedtime.

The snow melted, and life resumed its pace, but Serena was different. The snowstorm hadn't just stopped the town; it had reset Serena's compass.

Months later, as spring blossomed and Serena graduated, she thanked God for that snowy day. Her journey, echoing Mary and Martha's story, underscored the importance of holding onto faith even when life's demands pull you in different directions. Amidst the celebrations, she wrote

70

in her journal, "In the stillness, I found my path. Gratitude for snowfall and second chances."

Daily Dose of Faith

Set specific times during your day for prayer or meditation. It could be a short morning prayer, a midday gratitude pause, or a nighttime reflection. Remember the devotion of Mary and Martha through their struggles; consistency helps in ensuring you don't neglect your spiritual nourishment.

Living the Faith

Here's another example to consider. Jamie had a busy schedule, but every Wednesday, she'd attend a prayer group. It became her anchor, helping her stay grounded. Much like Mary and Martha, Jamie learned to prioritize her faith while navigating life's challenges. The fellowship reminded her that amongst the chaos, her faith community was a constant source of support.

Journal Time!

* Reflect on a week when you felt overwhelmed by responsibilities. What were your main stressors?

* How do you ensure your faith isn't overshadowed during busy times?

* Drawing from Mary and Martha's story, how do you think they managed their faith and duties?

* Recall a time when your faith provided solace during a demanding period. Describe that experience.

Wrapping Up the Week

Life is a juggling act, and at times, the balls you're juggling seem too many. But with faith and persistence, you can find a balance that honors God, your commitments, and your well-being.

Week 14: Make Wise Choices

Who is wise and understanding among you? Let them show it by their good life, by deeds done in the humility that comes from wisdom.

—James 3:13

Recommended Reading:
The story of King Solomon (1 Kings 3:3–28)

Every day, you make countless choices—from simple decisions like what to wear to profound ones that shape your future. Much like King Solomon, your choices reflect what you value most. This week, focus on making choices aligned with wisdom and faith.

King Solomon, when offered anything he desired by God, chose wisdom over riches, long life, or the defeat of his enemies. This divine wisdom led Solomon to make just and enlightened decisions, earning him respect and solidifying his legacy as one of the wisest kings in history.

Your True Self

While King Solomon lived in a different era, the weight of making choices is a timeless struggle. In our digital age, with its myriad influences and opportunities, you probably grapple with decision-making. Solomon's choice to seek wisdom from God provides you with an exemplary role model. The fear of missing out, peer pressure, and societal expectations can cloud judgment. In these times, seeking wisdom is more crucial than ever.

Decisions at Dawn

Abeni had always been methodical, plotting her path meticulously. College, internship, job, promotion—it was all mapped out. So, when the letter from Hartman & Co., one of the most esteemed firms in the city, slid through her mailbox, offering her a summer internship, it should have been a moment of victory. And it was, until another letter arrived the next day.

Folded neatly was an invitation for a mission trip to a small village in Guatemala. Just as Solomon faced a defining choice, so did Abeni. The images of children with hopeful eyes, women carrying jugs of water, and verdant landscapes flashed in her memory. A presentation about this mission trip had been made at her college a month ago, and Abeni had felt an inexplicable connection.

Two letters. Two opportunities. But for Abeni, it felt like a divergence of two lifetimes.

Each night after dinner, she'd sit on her porch swing, the letters in her hands, weighing the pros and cons. She pondered deeply, much like Solomon did when presented with God's offer. The internship was a direct ticket to a successful career. It was what she had worked for and what everyone expected of her. The mission trip, on the other hand, was unpredictable. There was no tangible benefit, no guaranteed success story at the end of it. Yet, whenever she closed her eyes, she saw the village, heard the children's laughter, and felt the warmth of a community she had never met.

Her friends were split in their advice. "Think about your future," said Jenna, always practical. "Sometimes, it's not about the resume. It's about the heart," mused Ben, who had spent a summer in Tanzania.

A conversation with her older sister, a wise woman who had seen the highs and lows of life, proved pivotal. On a lazy Sunday afternoon, as they potted plants together, Abeni spilled her dilemma. Tina, wiping dirt from her hands, said, "When I was your age, I stood where you are now. I chose the predictable, the safe. It was good, but I always wondered about the path not taken. Life is short, darling. Choose the journey that'll give you stories, not just milestones. Choose with wisdom, as Solomon did."

That night, Abeni dreamt of the village. She was teaching kids, laughing with the locals, and there was a sense of purpose and belonging.

Morning brought clarity. She called the mission's coordinator, her voice firm, "I'm in."

The summer in Guatemala wasn't easy. There were language barriers, bouts of homesickness, and days of sheer exhaustion. But there were also moments of profound connection, joy, and a deep understanding of humanity. Abeni discovered skills she didn't know she had, like leadership, empathy, and resilience.

When she returned, her skin was tanned, her backpack worn out, but her eyes—they sparkled with stories.

Hartman & Co. did come around the following year, offering her another internship. This time, Abeni accepted, but she was a changed person. The boardroom and the village, both had lessons to offer, and Abeni was keen on embracing them all.

As the years passed, Abeni climbed the corporate ladder, her experiences in Guatemala enriching her personal and professional journey. One day, in her corner office, a simple photograph claimed the place of honor—Abeni surrounded by Guatemalan kids, their smiles wide, their spirits free. A testament to a summer of choices, and much like King Solomon's legacy, it was a testament to the power of divine wisdom in guiding those choices.

Daily Dose of Faith

Whenever you face a decision, big or small, pause and pray for guidance. Remember how Solomon sought God's wisdom; you too can turn to Him for insight. God's wisdom is always available to those who seek it. Also, surround yourself with wise counsel; confide in those who walk in faith and have your best interests at heart.

Living the Faith

Here's another example to consider. When confronted with tough choices, Tessa would always ask herself, "What would bring me closer to God's purpose for my life?" This simple question helped her make decisions that enriched her journey with Christ. It's a reminder that, like Solomon, you can align your choices with a higher purpose.

Journal Time!

* Reflect on a recent choice you made. How did you come to that decision, and how did it make you feel afterward?

* What does wisdom mean to you? How do you recognize it in others?

* Inspired by Solomon's story, if God offered you anything your heart desired, what would you ask for and why?

* Think about a decision you're currently facing. How can you seek God's wisdom in this situation?

Wrapping Up the Week

As you reflect on Abeni's journey and Solomon's wisdom, it becomes evident that choices, big or small, shape your life. Seeking God's wisdom offers clarity and purpose amid life's crossroads.

Week 15: Cultivate Gratitude

"Give thanks in all circumstances;
for this is God's will for you in Christ Jesus."
—1 Thessalonians 5:18

Recommended Reading:
The story of the ten lepers (Luke 17:11–19)

This week, you'll dive deep into the world of gratitude. You'll understand why saying "Thank you" to the universe and to those around you is not just a polite gesture but a pathway to joy and contentment.

In the Gospel of Luke, Jesus heals ten lepers, but only one returns to express gratitude. This singular act of thankfulness stands out, reminding you to be that one person who recognizes blessings and offers thanks. This story underscores the importance of expressing your thankfulness, both to God and to those who touch your life.

Your True Self

In today's fast-paced, comparison-driven society, it's easy to feel discontented, focusing on what they lack rather than what they possess. Like the nine lepers who forgot to express gratitude, it becomes easy to overlook the blessings before you. Gratitude offers a refreshing lens through which you can appreciate life's blessings, big and small.

The Summer of Gratitude

Paulette always wanted more from life. More followers on her social media, more popularity at school, more expensive brands hanging in her closet. The latest phone model in her hand was already seeming obsolete because there was a newer version advertised. She existed in a perpetual state of aspiration, and satisfaction was fleeting.

As summer approached, her parents surprised her with a decision. They hoped this change would help Paulette recognize and appreciate the many blessings she already had, much like the solitary leper who returned to Jesus with gratitude. Instead of the Europe trip she anticipated, she would be volunteering in a rural community, helping to set up a library for kids. Paulette was aghast. The mere idea of spending her summer without malls, her favorite coffee shops, and her social circle seemed like a nightmare. But her parents stood firm. They believed she needed a change in scenery, a different perspective.

The first few days of her volunteering stint were tough. The sweltering heat, the starkness of her surroundings, and the lack of immediate connectivity all felt alien and overwhelming. Paulette often found herself sitting on the porch of her homestay, missing the hustle and bustle of her city life.

But as days turned into weeks, subtle transformations began to unfold. Paulette noticed the children's eagerness to learn, their faces lighting up at the sight of new books. She watched families share modest meals, their homes open and hearts even more so. She saw other teens who, instead of fretting over the latest trends, found happiness in simpler pursuits—a game of soccer, a day at the river, or a night sharing stories under the starlit sky.

One evening, a young girl named Maya approached Paulette with a handcrafted bracelet. This simple gesture, reminiscent of the thankful leper, symbolized sincere appreciation. It was made of colored threads with intricate patterns. Maya explained that it was a token of gratitude. Her younger brother had started reading books from the library

Paulette helped set up, and it made a difference in his life. Tears glistened in Paulette's eyes as she wore the bracelet. It wasn't just an accessory; it was a symbol of the impact she had unknowingly made.

In the days that followed, Paulette witnessed the genuine camaraderie between the villagers and understood the joy in their simple routines. Paulette began to immerse herself in the community, not as a volunteer from a privileged background, but as an equal participant in their daily life. She helped in the fields, cooked with the local women, and played with the children. Every night, she'd write down her experiences in a diary, her words reflecting her evolving mindset.

As summer drew to a close, Paulette felt a heavy weight in her chest. The community she once viewed with apprehension had now become a place she held close to her heart. On her last day, the villagers organized a small farewell for her. Songs were sung, dances were performed, and heartfelt goodbyes were exchanged.

When Paulette returned home, her room seemed different. The numerous gadgets, the expensive dresses, the piles of makeup—they all appeared excessive. She realized that in the pursuit of "more," she had overlooked the abundance in her life.

The experience taught her gratitude. Paulette started practicing mindfulness, valuing moments over material possessions. Her transformation mirrored the journey from being like the nine lepers who took their healing for granted to the one who returned with a heart full of gratitude. She started a gratitude journal, where she'd write three things she was thankful for every day.

Over the years, while the colors of Paulette's bracelet faded, the memories and lessons it embodied remained fresh in her heart. It was a reminder of a transformative summer and a testament to the profound understanding that sometimes, less is truly more.

Daily Dose of Faith

Start each day by listing three things you're thankful for. It could be as profound as a supportive family or as simple as a warm bed. Over time, this practice will rewire your mind to focus on abundance rather than shortage.

Living the Faith

To further illustrate the power of gratitude, consider another real-life example. Zuri began keeping a gratitude journal after feeling overwhelmed with envy from scrolling social media. This simple act transformed her attitude, and she began to find joy in her daily life, realizing that she was immensely blessed in countless ways.

Journal Time!

* List five things you're deeply grateful for right now.

* Describe a time when you felt immense gratitude. What sparked that feeling?

* Considering the story of the ten lepers. What motivations or circumstances might have prevented the other nine from expressing their gratitude?

* Are there unsung heroes to whom you'd like to express gratitude? Jot down their names and why you're thankful for them.

Wrapping Up the Week

Just as the story of the ten lepers teaches, gratitude isn't just about acknowledging your blessings but actively expressing them. Gratitude is more than just an emotion; it's a lifestyle. As you focus on your blessings and express your thankfulness, you cultivate a heart that is content, joyful, and aligned with God's grace. Challenge yourself to live with an attitude of gratitude every single day.

Week 16: Grow in Your Faith Journey

"Therefore, since we are surrounded by such a great cloud of witnesses, let us throw off everything that hinders and the sin that so easily entangles. And let us run with perseverance the race marked out for us, fixing our eyes on Jesus, the pioneer and perfecter of faith."

—Hebrews 12:1–2

Recommended Reading:
The story of the apostle Peter (Matthew 16:13–20; 26:69–75; Acts 2:1–41)

Faith isn't a destination; it's a journey. Sometimes you soar, other times you falter, but always, you grow. This week, you'll delve deep into understanding the evolution of your faith journey and take inspiration from one of the most dynamic disciples: Peter.

Peter, initially known as a simple fisherman, underwent significant spiritual growth. Over time, through his experiences, mistakes, and unwavering belief, he became a cornerstone of Christianity. Though he denied Jesus three times, his repentance and unwavering dedication later show that it's not about how you start but how you grow, learn, and dedicate yourself to God's path.

Your True Self

You are navigating uncharted waters—full of emotions, questions, and changes. It's a phase where you can draw parallels with Peter's transformation journey. It's natural to face doubts and challenges in your faith journey during these transformations. However, these are also times of immense spiritual growth; just as the changes in your body and mind shape you, the fluctuations in your faith mold your spiritual self.

Unwavering Faith

One evening, seeking to understand her faith better, Clelie found herself in the church basement. She sat awkwardly on a wooden bench, feeling out of place. Around her, animated voices filled the room, recounting stories of profound spiritual experiences and meaningful encounters with faith. She fidgeted with the frayed edges of her jeans, feeling conspicuously out of place. It reminded her of Peter's initial uncertainty in following Jesus. Why had she even thought that joining the youth group would be a good idea?

It wasn't that Clelie didn't believe; it was just that she felt her faith was different. It wasn't as unwavering as others seemed to have it. She had questions, uncertainties, and an unsettling feeling of being adrift in a vast sea of believers.

One evening, after a particularly introspective session, Clelie stayed back, lost in thought. The youth leader, Mrs. Anderson, approached her with a gentle smile. "Is everything okay, Clelie?" she asked.

Clelie hesitated before confessing, "I just don't feel like I belong here. Everyone seems so...sure of their faith. And I'm just...not."

Sensing Clelie's discomfort, Mrs. Anderson sat down next to her. "You know, Clelie, even the strongest believers have had their moments of doubt. Much like Peter, who despite being so close to Jesus, faced his own struggles. Have you ever read about Peter in the Bible?"

Clelie shook her head.

Mrs. Anderson, with a comforting tone, said, "You know, Peter, one of Jesus's closest disciples, also grappled with his faith at times. But even he had his moments of doubt. He denied knowing Jesus three times before the rooster crowed, just as Jesus had predicted. Yet, after all his mistakes and doubts, he emerged as a pillar of the early church. His faith, though tested, never wavered in the end."

Clelie listened intently. Somehow, the story of a man who lived thousands of years ago felt relatable.

"In many ways," Mrs. Anderson added, "Peter's journey is a testament to the fact that faith isn't about being perfect. It's about growing, learning, and finding your way back even after you've lost it."

Clelie thought about the many times she'd read stories from the Bible and felt a disconnection, but today, the story of Peter gave her hope. Maybe she didn't need to have all the answers right away. Perhaps, like Peter, her journey was about navigating the ups and downs of faith.

With each passing session, Clelie began to see her doubts as part of her faith journey. Emboldened by this perspective, she started attending the group meetings with renewed vigor. She engaged in discussions, shared her doubts, and found that many others felt the same way. The youth group became a sanctuary for her—a place where she could be herself, doubts and all.

As the months rolled by, Clelie's relationship with faith transformed. She learned to see it not as a static entity but as a dynamic, evolving bond. Much like how Peter's relationship with Jesus evolved over time, so did Clelie's understanding of her faith. The story of Peter became her anchor, reminding her that faith was as much about the journey as the destination.

One evening, as Clelie shared her experience with a newcomer to the group, she realized how far she had come. From a place of doubt and uncertainty, she had found a home in the youth group, strengthened by the stories of those who had walked the path before her.

The youth group was no longer a place where Clelie felt out of place. It had become a haven, a space where she, like many others, learned that faith was a journey, not a destination. And in the story of Peter, she found solace, understanding that even in moments of doubt, one could find their way back to unwavering faith.

Daily Dose of Faith

As you reflect on Peter's journey and Clelie's experiences, look at a practice that can help bolster your own faith. Commit to spending ten minutes each day in quiet reflection. Whether it's reading scripture, praying, or simply meditating on God's word, remember Peter's transformation and know that faith can strengthen over time, this daily practice will fortify your faith, especially in times of doubt.

Living the Faith

Here's another example to consider. Lena always carried a small pocket Bible. Whenever she felt overwhelmed or uncertain, she'd find a quiet corner and read a verse or two. This habit became her anchor, grounding her faith even in turbulent times.

Journal Time!

* Reflect on a time when your faith was tested. How did you overcome that challenge?

* What practices or rituals help you feel closer to God?

* How do you relate to Peter's faith journey, from doubt to dedication? Consider the challenges he faced and how he emerged stronger in his faith.

* Imagine your faith journey as a path through a forest. Describe the scenery, challenges, and beautiful moments you envision.

Wrapping Up the Week

Growth often comes wrapped in challenges. Embracing your doubts, learning from your stumbles, and continually seeking God's guidance much like Peter did in his journey, will ensure that your faith journey, though winding, leads you closer to His eternal love. Just as Peter's faith journey was marked by growth and transformation, remember that every step you take, whether backward or forward, is a chance to grow closer to God.

Week 17: Understand God's Love

"For God so loved the world that he gave his one and only Son, that whoever believes in him shall not perish but have eternal life."

—John 3:16

> **Recommended Reading:**
> The parable of the prodigal son (Luke 15:11–32)

God's love is a light that never dims, no matter how far you drift. This week, you'll immerse yourself in one of the most touching parables Jesus told—the story of the prodigal son. Just as the prodigal son drifted away and later found his way back to his father's love, your story today mirrors that journey back home to the arms of those who care for you. Let's journey together into the heart of God's boundless love.

The parable of the prodigal son is a moving depiction of God's love. A son squanders his inheritance and lives a reckless life, only to find himself destitute. When he decides to return home, expecting anger and retribution, his father welcomes him with open arms, symbolizing God's unfailing love for you, no matter your transgressions.

Your True Self

In a world increasingly dominated by social media likes, where fleeting friendships and peer pressures often shape your perceptions, understanding the essence of true love can become challenging. But remember, God's love isn't based on conditions or standards. It is vast, unwavering, and always waiting for you, even when you falter. It's like the love the father showed his lost son in the parable, welcoming him back without judgment or reservation.

Homecoming

The old oak tree cast long shadows over the winding road leading to Claire's childhood home. The sight of that tree always gave her a sense of comfort, a marker that she was close to her safe haven. But today was different. Today, the shadows it cast seemed ominous, signaling a decision Claire was still wrestling with.

Two weeks ago, Claire had stormed out of that very home, her youthful determination convincing her that she was better off without the weight of her parents' expectations. An argument about her future, her choices, had reached its boiling point. With tear-filled eyes and an overstuffed backpack, she had made a rash decision to leave.

Claire sought refuge with Aurélie, an old friend from high school with whom she shared countless memories and secrets. She was convinced she'd find the freedom she yearned for away from her family's confines. But as the days turned into nights, Claire's initial feeling of liberation started to wane. Aurélie, although kind, had her own life, and Claire often found herself lying awake on the living room couch, engulfed by a profound sense of isolation. The laughter and chatter of her family, which she had once found stifling, now echoed in her memories, making her heart ache with longing. A familiar tale from scripture played in her mind, and she wondered if, like the wayward son, she could find her way back.

Every evening, she would walk to the edge of town, just close enough to glimpse that old oak tree in the distance. The warmth of her memories contrasted sharply with the cold reality of her situation. It was during one such evening that Claire's façade of stubbornness began to crack. The weight of her decision bore down on her. She yearned to hear her mother's comforting voice, to see her father's kind eyes. Her pride battled with her longing, but with every tear that streamed down her face, pride took a backseat.

Taking a deep breath, Claire decided it was time to face the consequences of her actions. She packed her belongings and set off toward home as the sun began to set. With every step she took, a whirlwind of emotions surged within her. What would they say? Would they even want her back?

As the familiar outline of her house came into view, Claire hesitated. She looked at the porch, half expecting to see it empty, a testament to the void she had created. But to her surprise, her parents stood there, their eyes fixed on the road, as if they had been waiting for her since the day she left. In their embrace, Claire felt the overwhelming love just as the prodigal son must have felt upon his return.

The next few moments felt surreal. The distance between them seemed to melt away as Claire took those final steps. Her mother's eyes welled up with tears, and her father's firm posture wavered with emotion. Without a word, they rushed toward her, their arms open wide.

The embrace was warm, protective, and filled with overwhelming love. Words were unnecessary. The tightness of the hug conveyed more than words ever could. The weight of regret, loneliness, and the fear of rejection lifted, replaced by relief, love, and a deep sense of belonging.

The argument that had once seemed so monumental now paled in comparison to the bond that Claire and her parents shared. In that moment, she realized that home wasn't just a place, but a feeling. This connection remained unbroken even in the face of adversity.

Daily Dose of Faith

Every morning, remind yourself of God's love by reading a Bible verse about His affection. This simple act will anchor your day in the knowledge that you are eternally cherished. Reflect on the parable of the prodigal son—God's love is always awaiting your return.

Living the Faith

Here's another example to consider. Katie cherished a small pendant, a gift from her uncle, inscribed with "Loved beyond measure." She'd clasp it in moments of doubt or sadness, drawing strength from its message. It served as a tactile reminder of God's love, echoing the sentiments of the father in the parable of the prodigal son.

Journal Time!

* Reflect on a time you felt distant from God. What brought you back to His embrace?

* How do you personally experience God's love in your daily life?

* In what ways can you show others the kind of unconditional love God offers us?

* Write a letter to God, expressing your understanding and gratitude for His love.

Wrapping Up the Week

As you've seen from the tale of Claire and the parable itself, God's love remains steadfast, offering a sense of belonging and understanding. It isn't something you earn but a birthright that envelopes you. Move forward with the knowledge of this love, sharing its warmth and compassion with those you encounter.

Week 18: Live with Integrity

"Whoever walks in integrity walks securely,
but whoever takes crooked paths will be found out."
—Proverbs 10:9

Recommended Reading:
The story of Tamar (Genesis 38)

Integrity is not solely about honesty; it's about living authentically and upholding values, even in the face of adversity. This week, you'll immerse yourself in Tamar's story—a testament to determination and the pursuit of justice. Tamar's life lessons remind us that maintaining one's integrity might challenge societal norms, but it's this very path that manifests God's blessings and protection.

In a society dictated by patriarchal norms, Tamar stood out as a woman of courage and conviction. After being wronged by her father-in-law, Judah, and facing the possibility of a bleak future, she devised a plan to ensure her rights and secure her future. Her actions were risky, and she knew the consequences of being found out would be dire. However, Tamar held firm to her belief in justice and righteousness. When confronted, Judah himself admitted, "She is more righteous than I." Her story showcases that sometimes, the path of integrity is treacherous, but with faith and courage, it can lead to validation and honor.

Tamar's story is complex, and while some might find certain elements controversial, it's an essential narrative about a woman's determination to secure justice and righteousness for herself, even in a society that often marginalized women.

Your True Self

In a world where societal expectations often overshadow personal truths, real integrity can sometimes feel elusive. Yet, holding fast to your beliefs and values, especially when they challenge the status quo, is essential. Tamar's story exemplifies this. It's about claiming justice, standing up for one's rights, and doing so with wisdom and resilience. Like Tamar, who remained unwavering in her quest for justice, you too can make choices that reflect your innermost convictions and values.

Choices at Crossroads

Zaidee's fingertips drummed on the library's wooden table. The final exam was less than twenty-four hours away. While her classmates huddled in groups, sharing notes and last-minute insights, Zaidee was grappling with a solitary dilemma. Much like Tamar, who was faced with a choice between her right to justice and societal norms, Zaidee was now in a situation where her values were tested.

While searching for an old notebook in the back shelves, she stumbled upon a crumpled paper. As she unfolded it, her heart skipped a beat. It was the answer key for tomorrow's exam, likely misplaced by a teacher or an assistant. The realization hit her: in her hands, she held the power to ace the most critical test of the year. She pondered what Tamar would do in her place, considering her determined stand for justice.

Zaidee had always been a diligent student. Late-night study sessions and meticulous notes were her rituals. She took pride in her hard work and the grades she earned. But this year had been challenging. Personal issues had divided her attention, and her preparation for the finals hadn't been as thorough as she'd have liked. The allure of the answer key was undeniable. With it, she could easily ensure a top grade, safeguard her scholarship, and glide into the summer.

But as the hours passed, the weight of the decision pressed on her. Zaidee thought of her younger brother, Jack, who always looked up to her. Would she be able to face him if she took this shortcut? She remembered her mother's words, "Integrity is doing the right thing, even when no one is watching." Did she want success at the cost of her self-worth? She realized that like Tamar, she was facing a test of character.

Night deepened, and the library's lights dimmed one by one. Zaidee sat alone, the answer key a silent temptress beside her. She visualized herself walking into the exam hall, the secret knowledge burning a hole in her pocket. She could almost feel the weight of the guilt she'd carry, the hollowness of a victory unearned. Drawing inspiration from the story of Tamar, she knew she couldn't compromise her integrity.

With sudden clarity, Zaidee made her decision. She would not let this paper define her worth or her future. She took out a pen and scribbled a note on the answer key. "Found this. Please be more careful next time." She slipped the paper into a plain envelope and dropped it into the teacher's mailbox.

The following day, the sun streamed into the classroom as Zaidee took her seat, her nerves taut but her conscience clear. The questions were challenging, and while she wasn't sure of every answer, she was confident that she had given it her all. The satisfaction of honest effort was more gratifying than any guaranteed A+. Her choice echoed the strength and steadfastness of Tamar's choices in ancient times.

A few days later, as the grades were posted, Zaidee felt anxious. But when she saw her score—a respectable B+—a genuine smile spread across her face. It was a testament to her hard work, resilience, and most importantly, her integrity. Through this experience, Zaidee had learned first-hand the value of staying true to oneself, a lesson she shared with the biblical figure, Tamar.

Word soon got around about the misplaced answer key. While no one knew who had returned it, whispers of admiration filled the hallways. Zaidee kept her role a secret, choosing to cherish the personal victory of her choice. But in her heart, she knew that the real test had been outside the exam hall, and she had passed with flying colors. This victory was not just about academics; it was about personal integrity, a value that the story of Tamar exemplified.

Daily Dose of Faith

Every evening, reflect on your actions of the day. Were they aligned with your values? It's never too late to apologize, correct, or make a different choice tomorrow. Let the story of Tamar remind you that integrity is not only a personal virtue but also a spiritual one.

Living the Faith

Here's another example to consider. Jazmin faced a common dilemma among her peers: attending a party where she knew some activities might go against her beliefs. She wrestled with the fear of missing out and the desire to fit in. Yet, recalling Tamar's story, she chose to prioritize her values and instead, hosted an evening with close friends that aligned with her principles.

Journal Time!

* Recall a time you faced a moral dilemma. How did you handle it, and how did it make you feel?

* In what areas of life do you find it most challenging to maintain your integrity? How can you strengthen it?

* How does maintaining integrity strengthen your relationship with God?

* Commit to one specific way you'll uphold your integrity this week. Consider how Tamar's unwavering determination can inspire and guide you in your personal commitments.

Wrapping Up the Week

Integrity guides your actions and decisions, leading you to an authentic, meaningful life. By choosing to live with honesty and authenticity, you honor yourself and reflect the values God instilled in you. Let Tamar's story inspire you to be brave, be true, and shine brightly in your integrity. Just as her determination led her to justice, your commitment to truth and authenticity can open doors and bring blessings into your life.

Week 19: Encourage Others

"Therefore encourage one another and build each other up, just as in fact you are doing."
—1 Thessalonians 5:11

Recommended Reading:
The story of Priscilla and Aquila mentoring Apollos
(Acts 18:24–26)

Encouragement can manifest in many forms, be it words of affirmation, acts of kindness, or sharing wisdom. Drawing inspiration from the New Testament, we come across the story of Priscilla and her husband, Aquila. When they encountered Apollos, a sincere and eloquent speaker in the synagogue, they realized that his understanding of God's way was not complete. Instead of dismissing him, they took him aside and explained the way of God more accurately. Their actions weren't merely instructional; they were deeply encouraging. By guiding Apollos, they showcased the power of constructive guidance and the importance of fostering growth in fellow believers. Priscilla's story, alongside her husband, reminds us that our knowledge, patience, and willingness to uplift others can transform their spiritual journey.

Your True Self

In a world quick to critique and judge, being a pillar of positivity can be revolutionary. Priscilla and Aquila demonstrated how genuine mentorship and support can illuminate the path for others. Self-consciousness and doubts might sometimes cloud your vision, but the right words of encouragement can reignite the flame of belief in your potential.

Sumi's Second Wind

Sumi's cleats dug into the muddy grass, breaths coming out in short bursts as she raced toward the goalpost. With every practice session, she could feel her dream of making the school soccer team slipping away. Sumi felt her dream fading. The last few sessions had been nothing short of a disaster—missed shots, inaccurate passes, and dwindling confidence. Every miss, every error seemed to pile up in her mind, creating a wall that whispered: Maybe this isn't for you.

One evening, after another grueling practice, Sumi slumped on the bleachers, her head buried in her hands. Each time she closed her eyes, she could see the soccer ball darting right past the post, an inch away from a goal. The image was like a cruel loop, replaying her misses over and over.

That's when Ava, her longtime friend who had seen her through many highs and lows, found her. In that moment, Ava became Sumi's Priscilla, extending a hand of encouragement. Ava didn't say a word. Instead, she just sat next to Sumi, her presence a silent comfort. After a few minutes, Ava slipped a folded note into Sumi's hand and left, leaving Sumi curious.

Under the dim light of the field, Sumi unfolded the paper. The note was simple but profound. Ava had penned down their shared memories—games where Sumi had showcased incredible skill, times when she had led their local team to victory, and moments where her determination had shone brighter than any star player's talent. Ava wrote about how Sumi had always inspired her, how she believed in her when Sumi couldn't believe in herself. It ended with: "Remember, champions are made of courage, not just scores. You've got this."

Sumi's eyes welled up, feeling the pure essence of encouragement as she read and reread the note. Much like Priscilla's unwavering support to the early church and believers, Ava's words became Sumi's anchor. It wasn't about soccer or the team; it was about believing in herself. It was about not letting a few bad days define her journey. She clutched the note, taking a deep breath. Maybe I've been too hard on myself, she pondered.

The next practice was different. Sumi didn't carry the weight of her past failures; instead, she carried Ava's words in her heart. She felt more in tune with the game with every kick and pass. The coach, noticing this change in Sumi's spirit, gave her another chance at the goal.

This time, the ball soared past the goalkeeper, hitting the back of the net with a satisfying thud. Sumi's elated teammates surrounded her, but her eyes sought out Ava, who stood at a distance, clapping with a beaming smile.

The day the team list was put up, Sumi's name was on it. She had made it. But more than the victory, it was the journey, the belief, and the unwavering support of a friend that mattered most. As the team celebrated, Sumi pulled Ava into a tight hug, whispering a heartfelt thank you.

The season that followed was filled with highs and lows, but Sumi played with unbreakable vigor. Because now she understood. Sometimes, the most memorable goals aren't those scored on a field. They are achieved through resilience, backed by the power of uplifting words.

Daily Dose of Faith

Each day, make an effort to say something encouraging to at least three people—be it a friend, a family member, or even a stranger. It might be a compliment, a word of appreciation, or a motivational quote. In doing so, channel the spirit of Priscilla, touching lives and igniting hope.

Living the Faith

Here's another example to consider. Aiko started a chain reaction in her school by creating an "Encouragement Board" where students could pin notes of positivity for others. This act was a beautiful embodiment of Priscilla's spirit, illustrating the impact one small act can have on a community.

Journal Time!

* Think of a time when someone's encouragement made a difference in your life. How did it make you feel?

* How do you typically react when someone around you feels down or defeated?

* In what creative ways can you spread encouragement in your community or school?

* Reflect on the story of Priscilla. How can you embody her spirit of encouragement in your daily life? The consistent, genuine gestures can turn someone's world around.

Wrapping Up the Week

As you reflect on the importance of encouragement, challenge yourself to be someone's Priscilla this week. Encouragement isn't just about cheering someone on; it's about recognizing and illuminating potential. You light up the world by lifting others and celebrating their successes, one heart at a time.

Week 20: Be a Light in the World

"You are the light of the world. A town built on a hill cannot be hidden. Neither do people light a lamp and put it under a bowl. Instead they put it on its stand, and it gives light to everyone in the house. In the same way, let your light shine before others, that they may see your good deeds and glorify your Father in heaven."

—Matthew 5:14–16

Recommended Reading:
Matthew 5:14–16

You carry an undeniable, incredible spark within you. It's the light of kindness, courage, and faith. Just as Jesus highlighted the importance of being the light to His disciples, you too have this innate ability to shine in the darkest of moments. This week, delve into what it means to shine brightly, even in moments of darkness.

In Matthew 5:14–16, Jesus reminds his disciples of their vital and radiant role in the world. He urges them to shine, ensuring their deeds brighten the lives of others and glorify the heavenly Father. Layla's story that you're about to explore echoes this message. This message isn't just for the disciples; it's for everyone.

Your True Self

Do you sometimes feel like you're traversing a maze with only a flickering torch in hand? Peer pressures, school stresses, and personal doubts can overshadow your true self. Yet, like a town on a hill, your innate light has the power to cut through this darkness, guiding not just yourself, but others as well. But it's in these times that your inner light can shine the brightest, leading the way for yourself and others.

Layla's Lunch Bunch

Layla's footsteps echoed through the vast corridors of her new school, a rhythm that spoke of uncertainty and unfamiliarity. Layla yearned for a space where her light could shine. Students rushed past her—all immersed in their world of inside jokes, shared secrets, and familiar faces. To them, these walls felt like home, but to Layla, they were a sprawling labyrinth of solitude.

It wasn't just about being the "new girl." It was the stifling weight of sitting alone at lunch, the awkward silences in class group projects, and the slight sting of being the only one without weekend plans. There were moments, especially during those first few weeks, when the pangs of homesickness threatened to overwhelm her. But Layla, resilient and hopeful, wasn't one to be deterred.

One day, as she was settling into her usual corner in the cafeteria with her lunch tray, she looked around. Amid the animated chatter, she saw a few isolated islands—students like her, who sat by themselves, lost in their thoughts or books. Spotting them, Layla felt a strong pull, a desire to find her own light and help others shine. An idea began to form in Layla's mind.

The following week, a colorful poster appeared on the school's bulletin board: "The Lunch Bunch—Everyone's Invited! If you're looking for company, laughter, and a place to belong, come to the north end of the cafeteria. Let's eat together!" Beneath it, in Layla's neat handwriting, was the simple signature: "Started by someone who's been there."

The first Lunch Bunch meeting had only a handful of attendees. A quiet boy named Raj, who was passionate about astronomy. Maria, who had moved from Spain and missed her hometown's sunny beaches. And Rachel, a comic book enthusiast. Despite their varied interests, the common thread that bound them was the need for connection.

Layla's initiative wasn't an instant phenomenon. There were days when the group was small, and some where new faces appeared. But as days turned into weeks, something beautiful happened. As Jesus said that a lamp should give light to everyone in the house, Layla believed that everyone in the school deserved to feel warmth, love, and belonging. The Lunch Bunch began to grow, not just in numbers, but in its spirit.

Word spread, and students, both new and old, began to join. It wasn't just a table for those without company; it was a melting pot of stories, dreams, and laughter. Each member brought something unique to the table, be it a funny anecdote, a new game, or just a listening ear.

Soon, the Lunch Bunch wasn't limited to just lunches. They started organizing movie days, picnics, and study groups. The brilliance of the Lunch Bunch shone not because of one person but because of the collective light each member brought. Just as Jesus taught, when you let your light shine, others are inspired to do the same. The north end of the cafeteria buzzed with energy, drawing in even those who once viewed it with skepticism.

But for Layla, the most poignant moment came months later when a shy freshman approached her. "Thank you," the young girl whispered. "I was dreading my first day, but knowing the Lunch Bunch was here made it easier." Her gratitude was a testament to the power of being a light for others, a living embodiment of Jesus's teachings.

Layla's transformation from a newcomer to an inspiration of hope showcases the universal strength found in vulnerability. By reaching out, she not only found friends but also built a haven for many others like her. The hallways of the school, once daunting, now echoed with a different sound for Layla—one of belonging, unity, and the beautiful hum of friendship.

Daily Dose of Faith

Each morning, as you begin your day, light a candle, switch on a small lamp, or simply take a moment of reflection. Let it serve as a visual reminder of your purpose—to be a light. This act serves as a metaphorical stand for your lamp, a commitment to let your light shine and ensure it's visible, just as Jesus taught. Aim to perform at least one act of kindness daily, illuminating the path for someone else.

Living the Faith

As another shining example in line with Matthew's verses, Tara sought to illuminate the lives of her peers. Neddy initiated a project called "Letters of Light." She encouraged peers to write anonymous uplifting notes to others. These notes were distributed randomly, and the joy they spread was immeasurable. Tara showed that even simple acts can shine brilliantly.

Journal Time!

* Recall a time when someone else's "light" made a difference in your day. How did their action impact you?

* In which situations do you find it challenging to shine your light? Why?

* List three ways you can be a light in your school or community.

* Reflect on Matthew 5:14–16. What does it mean for you, personally, to be a "light" in the world?

Wrapping Up the Week

Being a light doesn't mean you have to shine intensely every moment. Much like the lamp mentioned by Jesus, it's about being consistent, visible, and guiding others through their own darkness. Each act of kindness, understanding, and love reinforces the divine light within you. As you journey forward, shine unapologetically, for you are indeed the light of the world.

Week 21: Practice Contentment

"I know what it is to be in need, and I know what it is to have plenty. I have learned the secret of being content in any and every situation, whether well fed or hungry, whether living in plenty or in want."

—Philippians 4:12

Recommended Reading:
The story of Paul's contentment (Philippians 4:11–13)

In a world where social media often showcases the idealized lives of others, making your own feel inadequate, it's challenging to feel content. It's easy to get swayed by external factors and forget Paul's lesson of finding contentment in Christ, regardless of your external circumstances. But what if contentment isn't about having everything but cherishing what you have?

Paul, in Philippians 4:11–13, speaks of learning contentment in any circumstance. Whether in need or in plenty, he found strength through Christ. Paul's words highlight a crucial difference between complacency, which is passive acceptance, and true contentment. The latter stems from an inner peace anchored in your relationship with God, not in fleeting worldly possessions. It's about grounding your satisfaction in a source that is unchanging.

Your True Self

Today's world, especially with the influence of social media, bombards you with images of "perfect" lives, making it easy to focus on what's missing rather than what's present. Just like Paul's message teaches you, it's essential to find peace and joy in your own journey, without constantly comparing it to others. However, recognizing the abundance in your life and practicing gratitude can shift your perspective from longing to contentment.

Daphney's Digital Detox

Daphney's mornings were predictable. The moment her alarm rang, her hand reached for her phone, opening the familiar app where a cascade of posts awaited her. With every scroll, she dove deeper into a world of curated moments: friends getting promotions, flaunting designer dresses, or sipping cocktails on pristine beaches.

She loved her friends and felt genuine happiness for their successes, but each post also sowed a seed of insecurity. Daphney's apartment view wasn't a beach but an alleyway. Her clothes, though cherished, bore no designer tags. It felt like life was a race, and while everyone surged ahead, she was still trying to tie her shoelaces.

One evening, after a particularly envious viewing of a friend's European getaway, Daphney felt an unfamiliar hollowness. The digital narratives she consumed daily began to blur the lines of her reality. She started measuring her self-worth by the weight of what she didn't have instead of valuing the treasures she did.

It was her stepfather's wise words that echoed in her mind: "Sometimes, to see clearly, one must close their eyes." Inspired, Daphney decided to embark on a week-long digital detox.

The first day was tough. The habit was so ingrained that she instinctively reached for her phone, longing for the familiar rhythm of scrolling. But she resisted. Instead, she bought a beautiful leather journal. Its crisp, empty pages seemed inviting, waiting for her to pen her story.

Every evening, Daphney started jotting down three things she was grateful for. Small details at first: a peaceful morning, her favorite song on the radio, a compliment from a colleague. But as days passed, her entries grew richer, reflecting deeper introspections.

Midweek, she wrote about her joy when an old friend called to reminisce about their college days. Another entry was dedicated to her satisfaction from helping a junior at work. Her journal became a testament to the myriad moments of joy that filled her days, previously overshadowed by the glamorous tales of her digital world.

By week's end, Daphney had not only filled several pages of her journal but also discovered spaces in her heart she hadn't known were empty. In her pursuit, she mirrored Paul's realization—that contentment isn't about external abundance but recognizing and valuing internal blessings. She logged into her social media, this time posting a photo of her journal, its pages filled with her neat handwriting. The caption read: "Counting blessings. Realized I have more than I ever recognized. Contentment is a perspective."

The likes and comments started flowing in, but Daphney's newfound clarity was not swayed by them. Among the hundreds of heart emojis, thumbs up, and comments, one stood out: "Inspired by you, starting my journaling journey tonight."

In her quest for contentment, Daphney found her peace and became an unwitting model for others. She embodied Paul's teachings, showing that true contentment comes from within and recognizing the blessings you already possess. The digital realm, with all its shimmer, had its place, but Daphney had discovered the beauty of pen and paper, of reflection, and of cherishing life's quiet, unfiltered moments. She had unearthed the simple truth that happiness is not a destination on a map but a lens through which one views the journey.

Daily Dose of Faith

Here's another example to consider. Laurel organized "Gratitude Gatherings" in her community, where people would come together in a relaxed setting, perhaps over tea and snacks, to share and listen to stories of gratitude. This not only fostered a sense of community but reminded everyone of the little joys often overlooked. These gatherings resonated with Paul's message, emphasizing contentment and gratitude.

Start a "Contentment Jar." Every day, jot down one thing you're content with and drop it in the jar. When you're feeling down or desiring more, read the notes to remind yourself of the blessings already in your life. This exercise helps ground you in the present moment, just as Paul encouraged believers to find contentment in every situation.

Journal Time!

* List five things you're genuinely content with in your life right now.

* Reflect on a time you felt discontent. What caused this feeling, and how did you cope?

* How does Paul's message in Philippians relate to your understanding of contentment?

* In today's digital age, what are some strategies you can employ to practice contentment?

Wrapping Up the Week

Contentment isn't a milestone you reach, but a path you choose to walk every day. It's a lesson Paul learned and shared with believers, emphasizing that your joy should not be rooted in the world's ever-changing circumstances but in the unwavering love and promise of Christ. It requires daily practice, gratitude, and a deep understanding that your value isn't determined by possessions or achievements but by God's unending love for you. In the words of Paul, let's find strength in Christ and cherish the blessings in every moment.

Week 22: Deal with Doubt

"But when you ask, you must believe and not doubt,
because the one who doubts is like a wave of the sea,
blown and tossed by the wind."

—James 1:6

> **Recommended Reading:**
> The story about John the Baptist (Matthew 11:2–6)

Doubts, questions, and uncertainties are natural parts of any journey, especially a faith journey. Having doubts doesn't signify a weakness in your faith; often, it reflects a deep engagement and connection with it. As with John the Baptist, moments of doubt can lead to a deeper understanding and affirmation of one's beliefs. Let's dive deep into understanding and navigating doubt together.

In Matthew, while John the Baptist was in prison, he sent messengers to ask Jesus if he truly was the Messiah. Even John, a prophet and the forerunner of Christ, had moments of doubt. Jesus responded not with condemnation but with evidence of His works and teachings, reassuring John in his faith.

Your True Self

In this age of information and rapid change, it's natural for you to face questions and doubts about many aspects of life, including faith. Just as John sought answers in times of uncertainty, so too can you today.

The key is not to suppress these feelings but to approach them with curiosity and a desire to understand.

Clarisse's Journey of Faith

Clarisse's earliest memories were threaded with hymns, the warmth of church gatherings, and Sunday dinners revolving around reflections from the morning's sermon. Her faith was as natural as breathing, handed down through generations. But as she stepped into the buzzing hallways of her high school, those pillars she'd always leaned on began to wobble.

High school was a melting pot of diverse ideas. Her physics teacher spoke of the Big Bang, her history teacher of wars fought in the name of faith, and her new friends came from various beliefs and backgrounds. Lunchtime discussions ranged from existential musings to the latest pop culture references. Clarisse, with her church-rooted views, often felt out of depth.

One evening, as she sat with her friends under the vast expanse of the starry sky, their talk meandered to the mysteries of the universe. Among her friends, Ryan often talked about his passion for astronomy, sharing tales of distant galaxies, while Zoe, proud of her cultural heritage, shared stories of reincarnation. During the exchange of beliefs, Clarisse felt a lump in her throat, unable to voice her feelings or even make sense of them.

That night, in the quiet of her room, Clarisse grappled with the questions that had been simmering within her. Was her faith too narrow? Did it leave space for the vastness of the universe? And the weightiest question of all was whether she was betraying her family's legacy by even entertaining such doubts?

The next Sunday, as Clarisse sat in the familiar wooden pew, she felt detached. It reminded her of how John the Baptist might have felt in his cell, questioning and seeking clarity. The sermon, the hymns, all felt distant, as if she was looking at them through a fogged-up window. After the service, Mrs. Jenkins, a kind old lady from the congregation, noticed her desolate look. "Tea at my place?" she offered with a knowing smile.

Sitting in Mrs. Jenkins's cozy living room, surrounded by the comforting aroma of fresh-baked cookies and a warm cup of tea in her hands, Clarisse poured out her heart. She spoke of her struggles, her guilt, and her fear of losing her faith. Mrs. Jenkins listened, her wise eyes never leaving Clarisse's face.

When Clarisse finished, Mrs. Jenkins took a deep breath, "You know, dear, faith isn't about never questioning. It's about seeking answers, wrestling with doubts, and coming out stronger."

She shared tales from her youth, of her struggles during the turbulent '60s, the cultural shifts, and how she too had questioned everything she'd known. "It's okay to question, Clarisse. Just as John the Baptist sought answers, it's through seeking that we truly find our path."

Emboldened by Mrs. Jenkins's words, Clarisse decided to form a group at school. In this open space, students could discuss their beliefs, doubts, and seek answers together. The group became a hit, drawing kids from diverse backgrounds. Drawing inspiration from their shared mission, they named the group "Seekers."

High school was filled with exams, proms, and graduation caps. But through it all, Clarisse found her anchor. She realized that faith wasn't a confining box but a river, always flowing and adapting. Her doubts didn't weaken her beliefs; they enriched them, adding layers of understanding and empathy.

Years later, as Clarisse stood in front of her congregation, now a youth pastor herself, she often spoke of her high school years, her doubts, and her journey back to faith. She would sometimes draw parallels between her own journey and John's, illustrating how both found reaffirmation after moments of doubt. Her story showed that it's okay to question, and that faith, like a river, finds its way even through the rockiest terrains.

Daily Dose of Faith

When doubts arise, don't push them away. Embrace them and discuss them with someone you trust—be it a pastor, a youth leader, or a friend. Reading related scripture and praying for guidance can also provide clarity. John the Baptist sought affirmation from Jesus; you can seek answers in your community and the Word.

Living the Faith

Here's another example to consider. When Juniace started college, she formed a group "Faithful Questioners." They would meet weekly, creating a safe space for anyone to share doubts and questions, and find answers together, strengthening their bond and faith.

Journal Time!

* Have you ever had doubts about your faith? What triggered these feelings?

* How did you feel when these doubts arose? Did you share them with someone?

* Reflecting on John the Baptist's story, what can you learn about dealing with doubt and seeking reassurance?

* How can you create a safe space for yourself and others to discuss and navigate doubts in faith?

Wrapping Up the Week

Doubts aren't a sign of weakness, but an indication of growth, exploration, and deep thinking. Even the strongest figures in the

Bible had moments of doubt. How you approach and navigate these doubts shapes your faith journey. Embrace the questions and seek the answers. Just as John found affirmation in his moments of doubt, you too can find strength and understanding in yours.

Radiant Faith

Week 23: Set Boundaries

"Above all else, guard your heart,
for everything you do flows from it."
—Proverbs 4:23 (NIV)

Recommended Reading:
The story of Queen Vashti (Esther 1:10–22)

Think of boundaries as invisible fences you set up to protect your heart, time, energy, and sanity. They are not barriers to keep others out, but guidelines that help you maintain your dignity and self-worth.

Just as Queen Vashti set clear boundaries by refusing to be paraded before the king and his guests, you must establish personal boundaries to safeguard your dignity and self-worth. Although called upon by King Ahasuerus during his feast, Queen Vashti declined his demand. Though it came at a personal cost, her refusal is a testament to the importance of standing up for oneself and setting clear boundaries, even when faced with immense pressure.

Your True Self

The push to conform, to be appreciated, and to fulfill expectations can make it challenging to stand one's ground. But, much like how Queen Vashti took a stance despite the consequences, you, too, must learn to assert your boundaries. This ensures you protect your integrity and remain true to your values, allowing you to be a better friend, student, and child of God.

The Art of Saying No

Mara's reputation was clear to everyone who knew her: if you needed something done, Mara was your go-to. In her own way, just as Queen Vashti was dedicated to her dignity, Mara was dedicated to hers—always being there for everyone. Whether it was volunteering for the school's annual bake sale, helping with a last-minute project, or simply lending an ear, she was always available. The word "no" seemed conspicuously absent from her vocabulary. In her heart, being the "yes girl" made her feel valued.

Mara's constant distractions mirrored how Vashti faced the expectations of the king and his court. Mara was constantly being pulled in every direction. One Wednesday, she found herself hurrying from a student council meeting to a friend's art showcase, all while mentally preparing a presentation due the next day. Her phone buzzed nonstop—texts from friends asking for study help, clubs requesting her presence, and reminders of commitments she'd made. By the time she flopped into bed, Mara felt more drained than fulfilled, the fatigue settling deep within her bones.

The next morning, as she hurriedly buttered her toast, her mother, Diane, took one look at her bleary-eyed daughter and made a decision. "Mara, after school today, we're having tea. Just you and me."

Mara wanted to protest—she had a thousand things lined up—but the firmness in her mother's eyes silenced any rebuttal.

That evening, the two sat in the kitchen, the aroma of chamomile wafting in the air. Diane began, "Do you know why I named you *Mara*? In many cultures, 'Mara' means strength and resilience. But strength isn't just about bearing loads. It's also about knowing when to set them down." Diane shared stories of her youth, moments she'd spread herself too thin, the burnouts, and the valuable lessons she'd learned about self-care and boundaries. "Life isn't about pleasing everyone, sweetie. It's about finding what truly matters to you and giving those things your best. The people who truly value you will respect your boundaries. And those who don't, well, do they really deserve all your yeses?"

The conversation was a revelation. Mara began to evaluate her commitments. She realized she'd said "yes" often out of fear—fear of missing out, of disappointing others, or not being seen as valuable. With her mother's guidance, she began the delicate task of setting boundaries. It wasn't easy. The first few "nos" were met with surprise, even disappointment. But as time went on, Mara noticed something incredible: she was happier, more focused, and even more effective in the commitments she chose to maintain.

Her friends, initially taken aback, began to understand and respect her choices. Some even confided they admired her courage to prioritize her well-being and wished they could do the same.

By the end of the school year, Mara, once always eager to please, had undergone a transformation. Her journey echoed Queen Vashti's: from challenges to firm decisions, and finally to a fulfilling resolution. She was still helpful, dependable, and there for her friends, but on her terms. She had discovered the power of boundaries, of intentional choices, and of understanding that sometimes, the most potent word one can say is a simple "no."

Daily Dose of Faith

* **Assess & Prioritize:** Understand what matters most to you.

* **Communicate Clearly:** Let those around you know your boundaries respectfully.

* **Stay Consistent:** It's easy to backtrack, but remember why you set these boundaries in the first place.

* **Seek Guidance in Prayer:** Whenever in doubt, turn to God's guidance in setting and maintaining your boundaries.

Living the Faith

Here's another example to consider. Drawing inspiration from Queen Vashti's story, when Asunción was asked by her friend group to join yet another club at school, she felt conflicted. Rather than going along with it out of obligation or societal expectations, Asunción paused to think about her own well-being and values. Remembering Vashti's courage in standing up for herself, Asunción took a deep breath and communicated her decision. Instead of an immediate yes, she evaluated her commitments and decided she needed time for herself and her faith journey. Her friends were surprised but came to respect her choice, and Asunción felt the reassurance that she was walking her authentic path.

Journal Time!

* List situations where you felt overwhelmed recently. Could setting boundaries, much like Queen Vashti did, have helped?

* How do you feel about saying "no" to someone? How might Vashti's courage inspire you to communicate your boundaries more effectively?

* Reflect on Vashti's decision to uphold her dignity. How can you apply her resolve in your life?

* Imagine a life with well-established boundaries. What does it look like?

Wrapping Up the Week

Setting boundaries isn't selfish; it's essential for personal growth and mental well-being. Like the boundaries Queen Vashti set for herself, which might have seemed like a rebellion but were vital for her self-respect, your boundaries safeguard your dignity and well-being. Embrace your values and stand firm in your decisions, ensuring you are at your best for God's work and yourself. Boundaries empower you to live with freedom and purpose. They allow you to embrace life's offerings with balance and grace. What's one boundary you'll commit to setting or reinforcing in your life this week?

Week 24: Overcome Temptation

"Watch and pray so that you will not fall into temptation. The spirit is willing, but the flesh is weak."
—Matthew 26:41

Recommended Reading:
The story of Jesus's temptation in the wilderness
(Matthew 4:1–11)

Temptation, a siren call that draws you toward choices you might regret. It's in the tiny moments, the decisions that challenge your morals and values, that your true strength is tested.

In the biblical account, after Jesus had been fasting for forty days in the wilderness, He encountered Satan, who presented Him with temptation. From turning stones into bread to jumping from a pinnacle, each temptation challenged Jesus's commitment to His mission and His trust in God. This story powerfully demonstrates that even the mightiest among us can be tempted; the true test is in your response. But with each attempt, Jesus responded with scripture, using God's word as a shield against temptation. In the end, Satan left, and angels came to attend to Jesus.

Your True Self

Living in today's world means navigating a maze of temptations—be it peer pressure, the allure of forbidden experiences, or the easier wrong over the harder right. Much like Jesus in the wilderness, you have values and teachings that can guide you through these trials. The key is not to avoid temptation but to learn how to overcome it.

A Test of Character

Leah's life was a series of neatly aligned dominos—meticulously planned, precisely executed. She was every teacher's pet, and her report cards gleamed with praise. Having garnered such a reputation, she felt a weight on her shoulders, an expectation to maintain the immaculate streak.

The challenge arose on a cloudy Wednesday. Just as Jesus faced challenges in the wilderness after days of fasting, Leah was confronted with her own wilderness of doubt. Algebra, the subject she once conquered with confidence, now stood like an unyielding wall before her. Quadratic equations seemed to dance mockingly on the pages of her textbook, eluding her comprehension. With a major test looming the next day, anxiety gnawed at her insides.

Her best friend, Mia, noticed Leah's distress during their lunch break. Glancing furtively around, Mia whispered, "Look, I've got something that might help." She discreetly slid a paper across the table. It was the answer sheet for tomorrow's test, complete with detailed solutions.

Leah stared, wide-eyed. The paper was tempting, much like the promises Satan made to Jesus. Here, on this innocuous sheet of paper, lay her salvation. It was the key to maintaining her academic perfection, a way out of the tight corner she felt trapped in. But then, a memory surfaced.

She was eight, sitting on her father's lap, listening to stories of integrity and honor. In the same way Jesus held onto scripture to combat temptation, Leah remembered her father's words that served as her moral compass. Her father would always say, "Character is who you are when no one is watching." That statement was etched deep within Leah's soul. She might not always understand algebra, but she understood values.

With a deep breath, Leah slid the answer sheet back to Mia. "I can't," she whispered, her voice firm. Mia looked incredulous. "But it's right here! No one will know."

Leah shook her head. "I would know, Mia."

The afternoon was a blur of scribbled notes, online tutorials, and practice problems. Leah worked hard, torn between her frustration and her determination to understand. She knew that the right path wasn't always the easiest, echoing the challenges Jesus faced during His temptations. The shadows grew long, and the night deepened. Leah, fueled by the decision she'd made at lunch, pressed on.

Morning dawned, and with it came the dreaded test. Leah walked into the classroom, sleep-deprived but with an undeniable fire in her eyes. As she worked through the problems, some answers flowed easily, while others required a deeper dig. But she persevered, relying on her preparation and refusing to let doubt cloud her judgment.

The days that followed were a blend of anticipation and dread. But when the graded tests were finally handed out, Leah felt a rush of emotions. Her grade wasn't perfect. It was a solid B. But the satisfaction she derived from that B was more profound than any A she had ever achieved.

Mia, who had aced the test with the illicit help of the answer sheet, looked at Leah's paper and scoffed, "Was it worth it?" Leah, clutching her test and with a small smile playing on her lips, simply said, "Absolutely."

After a class discussion about the ethics of cheating, Leah shared her experience, and word spread of her choice that day, and while some students didn't understand her decision, many viewed her with newfound respect. Leah had faced temptation and emerged with her integrity intact.

That test, while just a blip in her academic journey, became a defining moment in Leah's life. Just as Jesus emerged from the wilderness stronger and more resolved, Leah found strength in her decisions and values. It wasn't just about quadratic equations or algebraic formulas. It was a test of character, and Leah had passed with flying colors.

Daily Dose of Faith

* **Recognize the Temptation:** Begin by understanding what tempts you. Reflect on past situations where you've felt the pull, and be conscious of these triggers. Being aware is the first step.

* **Seek Strength in Prayer:** Whenever you feel tempted, turn to God for guidance and strength.

* **Avoid Temptation Triggers:** If certain situations or people consistently lead you into temptation, it might be wise to avoid them.

* **Accountability Partners:** Share your struggles with a trusted friend or family member who can support and guide you.

Living the Faith

Here's another example to consider. When Raquel, who had seen the adverse effects of alcohol on her family, was offered a sip at a party, she felt the weight of eyes watching her, expecting her to give in. But she thought of the promises she'd made to herself and politely declined. Later, she felt an overwhelming sense of pride, not for what she avoided, but for standing firm in her faith and values.

Journal Time!

* Reflect on a time you faced temptation. How did you handle it? What would you do differently now?

* How does Jesus's response to temptation inspire you?

* What are some "scriptures" or "principles" in your life that help you fend off temptation?

* Think of strategies you can use the next time you're faced with a challenging choice.

Wrapping Up the Week

Temptation is not a sign of weakness but an opportunity for growth. Like Jesus in the wilderness, you are equipped with powerful tools—faith, God's word, and an inner strength bestowed upon you. With these, you can face and overcome any temptation that crosses your path. It's not about never facing temptation, but about rising stronger each time you do.

Week 25: Learn from the Strength and Faith of Esther

"And we know that in all things God works for the good of those who love him, who have been called according to his purpose."

—Romans 8:28 (NIV)

Recommended Reading:
The story of Esther (Book of Esther)

Faced with the dire prospect of saving her people, Esther's courage shone through. Her story isn't just about bravery; it's about faith, understanding one's purpose, and the incredible things one can achieve when they trust in God.

Esther was an orphaned Jewish girl who became the queen of Persia. When a plan to destroy the Jews was set into motion by Haman, Esther faced a tough decision. Speaking out could cost her life. But with the guidance of her cousin Mordecai, and after fasting and praying for three days, Esther approached the king, revealing her Jewish identity and Haman's wicked plot. Her bravery and faith saved her people from destruction.

Your True Self

In today's world, where voices often get lost in the noise, it's common to feel overshadowed by age or lack of experience. But, just as Esther had her moment to rise despite her uncertainties, you might feel out of place or underqualified. It's God placing you in a situation not because you are ready, but because He is ready to work through you.

Bao's Stand

Bao was unlike most sixteen-year-olds at Jericho High. With her sharp wit, sense of responsibility, and deep empathy, it was no wonder she'd been elected to the student council. In some ways, her journey echoed that of Esther; both were young and in places of influence. She often found herself in rooms with seniors, their voices deep, confident, and occasionally dismissive of the young sophomore.

One cold December morning, the council members gathered for a meeting, coffee cups in hand. Bao, holding her hot cocoa, listened as the president unveiled the new plan: to repurpose the budget allocated for school clubs and redirect it toward upgrading the school's gymnasium. "Sports championships bring us trophies and elevate our school's reputation, attracting more funding and opportunities," he argued.

Bao's heart sank. The various clubs—from arts to robotics—provided solace, a haven for many students, an escape from the cacophony of school life. The implications of slashing their budgets were profound. It meant canceled events, stunted projects, and disheartened peers. Much like Esther, who recognized the dire consequences her people faced, Bao understood the stakes.

Later that day, in the quiet of her room, Bao's doubts weighed heavily on her. Who was she to oppose this? She was just a sophomore, after all. But then she thought of Esther, a young queen from her grandmother's stories. Despite her youth and the peril she faced, Esther took a stand to save her people from a sinister plan. She was scared, but she acted anyway because it was the right thing to do.

Bao clearly saw the parallels. Here she was, young and in a position of influence, faced with a decision that impacted many. Drawing a deep breath, she began her own plan.

Over the next few days, Bao engaged with students from different clubs, documenting their achievements, gathering testimonials on the clubs' impact, and taking photos of their activities. With the same fervor Esther had when advocating for her people, Bao prepared to present her case.

The day of the next council meeting arrived, and Bao's palms were sweaty. When her turn came, the room dimmed, and her presentation played. Vibrant images of drama club performances, intense robotics competitions, colorful art exhibitions, and soulful music recitals filled the screen. The determination in her voice was reminiscent of Esther's when she approached the king with her plea. Emotional testimonials from students echoed, speaking of friendships forged, skills learned, and safe spaces provided by these clubs.

As the lights came on, a palpable silence filled the room. Bao took a deep breath. "Our school's reputation isn't just built on sports. It's built on the diversity of talent and passion we foster in every corridor, every club, and every classroom. We have a responsibility not just to a selected few but to every student."

The days that followed were a blur of discussions and debates. The decision was finally reached: the budgets for the clubs would remain untouched.

Bao's bravery became the talk of the school. Students from all grades approached her, expressing gratitude, sharing their club stories, and even seeking advice on various matters.

In standing up for her peers, Bao hadn't just preserved the budget for clubs. She had, like Esther, harnessed the power of her position for the greater good. She reminds us that age does not define capability, and that, sometimes, the courage of one can spark change for many.

Inspired by Esther's valor and driven by her conviction, Bao had indeed made a difference.

Daily Dose of Faith

Esther's legacy provides key lessons that you can embrace today.

* **Embrace Your Position:** Just as Esther was positioned as a queen for a greater purpose, recognize where God has placed you.

* **Seek Wise Counsel:** Esther sought advice from Mordecai. Always surround yourself with wise individuals.

* **Fast and Pray:** Before making any significant decisions, take a moment to connect with God.

* **Be Courageous:** Know that God is with you, and take that step of faith even if you're afraid.

Living the Faith

Esther's spirit of courage reminds you of the bravery inherent in many of your actions. Here's another example to consider. Enma was torn about standing up for a friend who was being bullied. She felt alone in her fight, much like Esther. Drawing inspiration from Esther's courage, she reported the incidents to her teacher, started an anti-bullying campaign, and made her school a more welcoming place.

Journal Time!

* Esther's story has inspired many, just like Bao. Reflect on the lessons you can glean from her tale. What characteristics of

Esther's do you admire the most? Have you ever been in a situation where you had to stand up for what's right, even if it was scary? How can you apply the lessons from Esther's story in your everyday life? What's one courageous step you can take this week?

Wrapping Up the Week

Like many figures from scripture, you have a purpose, even if it remains veiled for a time. Esther's story shows you that sometimes you're placed in challenging situations not for you but for a greater purpose. With faith and courage, and trusting in God's plan, you can overcome fears and make a significant difference in the world around you.

Week 26: Develop a Heart for Worship

*"Let everything that has breath praise the Lord.
Praise the Lord."*
—Psalm 150:6

Recommended Reading:
The story of Mary in the house of Simon (John 12:1–8)

Worship isn't merely singing songs; it's expressing your deep love and adoration for God. Like Mary, when you bring your true self in worship, you create a connection with Jesus that is genuine and profound.

Mary entered Simon's house with an alabaster jar of expensive perfume. Without a word, she knelt by Jesus, breaking the jar and pouring the perfume on His feet. Then, with her tears and hair, she wiped them clean. Just as Mary showed her reverence in a pure and unfiltered act, you are called on to approach worship with authenticity. The act was criticized by many in the room, but Jesus defended her, recognizing her heart's genuine worship and devotion.

Your True Self

In a world filled with performance pressures, it's easy to get lost in doing things for appearances. Yet, as Mary's act shows, God values the sincerity of your worship more than any external display. God doesn't look at the show; He looks at the heart. Embracing an authentic heart for worship means stepping away from societal pressures and focusing solely on the divine connection.

Emily's Summer Awakening

Nestled among the whispering pines, Camp Living Waters echoed with the lively voices of teenagers, the strum of guitars, and the distant laughter from lakeside activities. Emily had arrived filled with anticipation for new experiences but also anxiety about fitting in. Yet, the spirit of worship, as exemplified by Mary's story, was about to touch her in a profound way. Camp was a new adventure and an unfamiliar terrain, far removed from her quiet suburban life.

Back home, Emily's Sundays were consistent; dressed in her Sunday best, she'd sit with her parents in their old wooden pew, listening to hymns sung in a measured tone. Worship was reverent, solemn, and structured.

But at Camp Living Waters, worship took a different form. There, under the open sky, campers displayed a passion for worship mirroring Mary's heart—arms raised and voices fervent. Emily watched from the fringes, hesitant and slightly uncomfortable. The open display of emotion seemed alien to her.

She tried participating, mouthing the words, but the weight of her own self-consciousness held her back. Every evening, as the campfire flickered and the stars shone brighter, she'd watch her peers lose themselves in worship, while she sat lost in her thoughts.

On the penultimate day of camp, Ms. Bennett, the camp's spiritual guide, narrated the story of Mary of Bethany. Emily listened intently as Ms. Bennett spoke of how Mary, in an act of uninhibited worship, broke her alabaster jar, pouring precious perfume on Jesus's feet and wiping them with her hair. Emily began to see parallels between Mary's bold act of worship and the freedom she witnessed in her fellow campers. It was a display of love, gratitude, and deep spiritual connection.

"True worship isn't about public display," Ms. Bennett said, "it's about genuine connection with God. It's not about where you are or how others perceive you; it's about the honesty of your heart."

Recalling Mary that evening, as the first chords of worship songs filled the air, Emily felt a pull. Mary's genuine and uninhibited act inspired her to overcome her barriers. Tentatively, she closed her eyes, letting the words wash over her. The world around her faded, replaced by the lyrics and their profound meaning. She began to sing, softly at first, then louder, each word echoing her feelings, doubts, and hopes.

As the chorus peaked, Emily felt a rush of emotion. Tears streamed down her face—not of sadness, but of realization, connection, and release. For the first time, she was not singing for others or going through the motions; she was singing for herself and God.

The last note hung in the air, but the change within Emily was palpable. When she finally opened her eyes, she was met with smiles and a few nods of understanding. Many had walked the same path of discovery, and they recognized the transformation in her.

The summer at Camp Living Waters ended, but Emily's spiritual journey had just begun. Her worship now echoed the same authenticity Mary had displayed. She returned home with a newfound understanding of worship, not as a ritual, but as a heartfelt connection. And while she still sat in the same old wooden pew, her approach to worship was forever transformed—genuine, heartfelt, and deeply personal.

Daily Dose of Faith

* **Seek Authenticity:** Worship in a way that feels genuine to you.

* **Understand Worship:** It isn't just about music; it's about connecting with God.

* **Private Moments:** Spend quiet moments in prayer, reflection, and worship.

* **Dive into the Word:** Engage with scriptures on worship to grasp its profound nature.

Living the Faith

Here's another example to consider. Jenna, a high school junior, started a worship group during lunch breaks. It began with just three friends and a guitar. Drawing from the heart of Mary's story, they focused on creating a space for genuine worship. Over time, more joined the group, drawn to the raw and sincere connection they felt there.

Journal Time!

* What does true worship mean to you?

* How do you express your love and gratitude to God?

* Have you ever felt judged or out of place during worship? How did you handle it?

* In what areas of your life can you invite God in more deeply through worship?

Wrapping Up the Week

True worship comes from a place of love, reverence, and genuine connection. Like Mary, who defied societal norms with her worship, when you prioritize your relationship with God over societal judgments or expectations, you experience a bond that is unbreakable and transformative. It's not about the act but the heart behind it.

Week 27: Practice Patience

*"But if we hope for what we do not yet have,
we wait for it patiently."*
—Romans 8:25

Recommended Reading:
The story of Job (Job 1:1–22 and Job 42:10–17)

Life's journey is filled with trials and tribulations. While it's easy to be impatient and wish for instant solutions, true strength and faith lie in waiting and trusting in God's timing, just like Job did.

Job was a man of immense faith and prosperity. However, he faced severe trials, losing his family, wealth, and health. Even with these calamities, and even with friends who questioned his integrity, Job did not curse God but exhibited immense patience. Ultimately, God restored his fortunes and blessed him even more than before.

Your True Self

In today's digital age, everything seems instant—messages, photos, even shopping. This immediacy can sometimes skew your perception of reality, making you more impatient. When faced with enormous trials, Job questioned why he was being tested so severely. Similarly, you can often feel impatient in your fast-paced world, wanting immediate clarity and results. Embracing patience means understanding that not everything in life is instant and that some of the most valuable things require time.

Sarah's Crucible

Just as ancient scriptures narrate the trials and tribulations of Job, you'll find modern parallels in your everyday lives. Consider Sarah, a high school student.

Sarah's room was a haven of order. Neat piles of books lined her shelves, post-its dotted her walls with reminders, and a study timetable meticulously planned her days. For as long as she could remember, Sarah had thrived in the structured world of academics. Her grades reflected her dedication: always perfect or near so. She wore her role of the "model student" as a badge of honor.

Then came her junior year of high school, and with it, a formidable adversary: Chemistry. From the first lesson, it felt like a different language. The periodic table appeared like cryptic runes, and balancing equations felt akin to solving ancient riddles. While she excelled in her other classes, Chemistry remained a persistent thorn in her side.

Determined, she sought help. Twice a week, after school, she met with Mrs. Carver, the Chemistry teacher, and on weekends, she enlisted the help of a tutor. But no matter how hard she tried, the perfect scores that came effortlessly in other subjects remained elusive. One particularly cold evening, after a grueling three-hour study session, she pulled out a test paper marked 72 percent. Tears blurred her vision. The weight of disappointment, exhaustion, and mounting pressure weighed on her.

Sarah contemplated dropping the class. Why invest so much time and energy into something that continually dragged her down? In her own way, Sarah's struggle with Chemistry mirrored the resilience that Job displayed during his tribulations. She shared her frustrations with her grandmother one Sunday afternoon, hoping for a sympathetic ear.

Her grandmother, always the storyteller, began recounting the tale of Job, a man of immense faith and patience. "Just like Job," her grandmother mused, "we all have our tests and trials, moments where our patience and faith are stretched to their limits." Despite losing everything and facing tremendous hardships, he remained steadfast and unyielding. His story wasn't about the losses he endured, but the strength of his character in the face of adversity. "Sometimes," her grandmother whispered, leaning closer, "our greatest lessons don't come from our successes, but from our struggles. It's not the outcome, dear, but the journey that molds us."

Sarah pondered those words. Inspired by Job's perseverance, Sarah began to recognize her own resilience. She remembered the countless hours she'd poured into understanding complex chemical reactions and realized that her growth wasn't reflected in the scores of her tests, but in the persistence she demonstrated. She may never top the class in Chemistry, but the resilience she was building was invaluable.

With renewed determination, Sarah dove back into her studies. Slowly, with each passing week, the subject began to unveil its secrets. She started to see patterns, to understand the logic, and to even appreciate the beauty in the bonds and reactions.

The school year eventually came to a close. Sarah received her Chemistry grade, an 85 percent. It wasn't perfect, and it certainly wasn't her highest score. But as she looked at the number, she felt an overwhelming sense of pride. The grade wasn't just a reflection of her understanding of Chemistry; it was a testament to her grit, her resilience, and her growth. In that journey, much like Job's, she understood the essence of patience and unwavering faith.

She had transformed, not with the flash and bang of an explosive reaction, but quietly, steadily, much like how a crystal slowly forms over time. And in that metamorphosis, Sarah found that sometimes, the most profound victories are those that don't show up as accolades or perfect scores, but as silent, indomitable strengths etched into one's character.

Daily Dose of Faith

* **Pause Before Reacting:** When faced with frustration, take a deep breath and pray for patience.

* **Remember Job's Resilience:** When struggling, recall how Job maintained his faith and patience through great trials.

* **Limit Instant Gratifications:** Consider practices like a digital detox, reducing impulse purchases, or setting aside deliberate "waiting periods" before making decisions.

* **Trust in God's Timing:** God's plan for you may differ from your timeline.

* **Reflect on Job:** Dive deep into his story whenever you need a reminder of profound patience.

Living the Faith

To further illustrate the importance of patience in your daily life, consider Maureen. She decided to grow a garden. Her friends laughed, knowing her penchant for instant results. Reminded of Job's patience in adversity, she took it day by day. Months later, not only did she have beautiful flowers and fresh veggies, but she had also cultivated an even more vital trait: patience.

Journal Time!

* Reflect on a time you showed patience. How did you feel afterward?

* In which areas of your life do you find it most challenging to be patient?

* How can you remind yourself to trust in God's timing during testing times?

* Connect with Job: How does his story inspire you when you face challenges?

Wrapping Up the Week

From Job's unwavering faith to Sarah's academic journey and Hannah's gardening, you see that patience is more than just waiting; it's about maintaining a positive attitude and growing in the process. In a world of immediacy, cultivating patience helps you grow spiritually, emotionally, and mentally. Take inspiration from Job and remain patient and faithful, knowing that God's plan is worth the wait.

Week 28: Prioritize Spiritual Growth

*"But seek first his kingdom and his righteousness,
and all these things will be given to you as well."*
—Matthew 6:33, NIV

Recommended Reading:
The story of Lydia who prioritized her spiritual growth
(Acts 16:13–15)

In your busy life, you might lose sight of spiritual growth. Lydia's story from Acts offers a timeless reminder of its importance. It's crucial to find a quiet space for your spiritual journey, just as Lydia did. Prioritizing spiritual growth provides a compass in the complexities of life.

In Acts, you learn about Lydia, a successful seller of purple cloth. Despite her bustling trade, she made time for spiritual reflection and growth. She didn't just hear Paul; she welcomed his teachings, providing an early base for Christian teachings in Europe.

Your True Self

Just as Lydia dedicated time for worship despite her busy career in trade, you too—despite your academics and extracurriculars—need that spiritual anchoring. In the race to "fit in" and meet expectations, your spiritual self can often be neglected. Yet, nurturing this facet can bring about peace, clarity, and purpose among chaos. Like Lydia, you can seek those moments of spiritual enlightenment even during the busiest phases of life.

Kalani's Quiet Hour

Kalani's life was frenetic. The smartphone that was perpetually clutched in her hand buzzed nonstop: texts from friends, reminders about soccer practice, updates about dance recitals, and of course, the endless stream of social media notifications. To an outsider, she was living the ideal high school life—popular, talented, and busy. But on the inside, Kalani felt like a hamster stuck on a wheel, constantly moving but never truly getting anywhere.

One evening, while aimlessly rummaging through her attic, she stumbled upon an old family Bible. The worn pages opened to the story of Lydia, a successful businesswoman from Thyatira, mentioned in the Acts of the Apostles. Drawing parallels to her own life, Kalani realized that even with a busy life, Lydia still prioritized her connection to God. Lydia, despite her demanding life, found time to seek spiritual nourishment. By a riverbank, away from the hustle and bustle of her daily commitments, Lydia dedicated time to prayer and reflection, eventually becoming one of the earliest European converts to Christianity.

The simplicity and dedication of Lydia's actions deeply resonated with Kalani. Seeing Lydia's commitment made Kalani wonder about her own spiritual priorities. Amid the chaos of ancient commerce, Lydia had carved out time for something more profound, something eternal. Kalani felt a profound need for such an anchor in her life.

The very next day, Kalani made a change. She decided that every evening, just before sunset, she would switch off her phone and spend thirty minutes in quiet reflection. This was her time—sacred and uninterrupted. Initially, it was a struggle. Her fingers twitched toward her phone, her mind raced with a list of tasks, and the siren song of social media beckoned. But day by day, the half-hour transformed from a challenge to a cherished routine.

With this newfound ritual, Kalani felt a weight lifting. Her problems, though they didn't disappear, seemed more manageable. Relationships grew deeper, not because she was constantly chatting, but because she was genuinely present in conversations. Much like Lydia's transformative moment by the river, Kalani had found her own space for spiritual growth. She began to understand herself better, discerning between what she wanted and what she truly needed.

One day, after a particularly grueling soccer practice, one of Kalani's teammates approached her. "You seem different," she remarked, "More...centered, somehow. What's your secret?"

Smiling, Kalani simply replied, "Half an hour."

Word spread, and soon, a few of her friends joined in, each finding their own quiet spot, their own half-hour of reflection. Drawing inspiration from Lydia's dedication, they began their own journeys of spiritual discovery. Together, they formed a bond, not over shared activities or gossip, but over shared spiritual growth.

Kalani's life remained busy, but the chaos no longer controlled her. Through her discovery of Lydia's story, Kalani realized that the need for spiritual grounding transcends time. Through dedicated moments of pause and reflection, Kalani had found clarity, purpose, and a deeper connection not just with the divine, but also with herself.

Daily Dose of Faith

* **Dedicate Time:** Even if it's just ten minutes, set aside time daily for prayer, meditation, or reading scriptures. Consider how Lydia, even with her responsibilities, made time for spiritual enrichment.

* **Join a Group:** Find or form a youth group at church or school to share and grow in your spiritual journey.

* **Digital Detox:** Dedicate a day or a few hours each week to unplug from digital devices, focusing instead on your spiritual practices. Use this time to connect with your spiritual self, much like Lydia did by the river.

* **Seek Mentorship:** Connect with someone mature in their faith to guide you, like how Paul mentored Lydia.

Living the Faith

Here's another example to consider. Anne-Caroline started a spiritual journal inspired by Lydia's dedication. Every evening, she'd write prayers, thoughts, and reflections. Over time, not only did her connection with God deepen, but she also understood herself better, leading to wiser decisions and a more contented heart.

Journal Time!

* How do you currently nurture your spiritual growth? Are there areas you wish to improve? Reflect on the distractions or barriers preventing you from deepening your spiritual journey.

* Think about Lydia and her commitment; how can you emulate that dedication in your own life? Inspired by Lydia, what steps can you take to make your spiritual growth a priority?

* How can your spiritual growth benefit others around you?

Wrapping Up the Week

Your spiritual journey is an anchor, offering solace, guidance, and perspective. While life's pace and demands can be intense, taking a cue from Lydia and making spiritual growth a priority can lead to a balanced, fulfilling, and purposeful life. As you wrap up the week, take inspiration from Lydia. In the week ahead, identify one action or habit you can introduce to prioritize your spiritual growth, ensuring it isn't overshadowed by life's demands.

Week 29: Trust in God's Timing

"For everything there is a season, and a time for every matter under heaven."
—Ecclesiastes 3:1, ESV

Recommended Reading:
The story of Sarah and Abraham waiting for Isaac
(Genesis 21:1–7)

There's a saying, "Good things come to those who wait." In today's age of same-day deliveries, binge-watching, and rapid information sharing, practicing patience can be challenging. Like Abraham and Sarah, you are sometimes asked to wait for the Lord's promises. The story of Sarah and Abraham is a testament to the beautiful outcomes that can emerge when you trust in God's timing.

In Genesis 21:1–7, Abraham and Sarah, despite being advanced in age and having faced years of barrenness, are blessed with a son, Isaac. God had promised them descendants as numerous as the stars. Though it seemed impossible, God's promise came true in His perfect timing.

Your True Self

The pressure to keep up, whether with trends, friendships, or life milestones, is immense. Like Sarah and Abraham discovered, your hopes and timelines might sometimes differ from God's intricate plan. This can lead to feelings of inadequacy or impatience. However, everyone's journey and timeline are unique, crafted perfectly by God.

Carmen's Waiting Game

Carmen's mailbox had become the center of her universe. Senior year was in full swing, and like clockwork, every afternoon after school, she would walk down the driveway, her heart pounding, hoping to find that thick, promising envelope from St. Augustine University, her dream school.

As days went by, her friends' joyous celebrations of college acceptances only intensified Carmen's sinking feeling, making her future appear more blurry in comparison. As she watched them joyously wave their letters, Carmen couldn't shake the stinging sensation of being left behind. She had the grades, the extracurriculars, the passion. So, why the silence?

One evening, while grappling with these thoughts, Carmen found herself at her grandmother's side, flipping through an old, worn-out family Bible. This wasn't just any story; it was one that mirrored her current feelings of longing and waiting. Drawn to a familiar theme of longing, she was engrossed in the story of Sarah and Abraham. Sarah had waited decades for a promise to be fulfilled, a child she thought she would never have. Abraham too had his doubts, thinking perhaps he had misheard or misunderstood God's plans. But in the end, the promise was kept, revealing a crucial lesson: sometimes, life unfolds in a divine sequence, which might not always align with your own timeline.

Her grandmother, noticing Carmen's immersion in the story, shared her wisdom. "When I was your age," she began, her voice soft and reminiscing, "I too waited for something precious. It was much like how Sarah and Abraham held onto God's promise even in the midst of doubt. It wasn't a college letter but a letter from your grandfather during the war.

Days turned into weeks, then months. But I held onto hope, just like Sarah did. And one day, the wait was over."

Carmen felt her grandmother's words deeply. Connecting with the story of Abraham and Sarah, she saw her journey in a new light. While agonizing, she realized that this period of uncertainty was also an opportunity to trust, grow, and understand that there's a more grand design at play—one that might not be immediately visible.

With this new perspective, Carmen found herself more at peace. She threw herself into her current commitments—leading a community service project, working on the school yearbook, and enjoying time with friends. Like Sarah's eventual joy in Isaac, Carmen began to trust that her moment of joy would come, in God's perfect timing. She started cherishing her final high school moments rather than wishing them away.

Then, on a crisp spring morning, it finally happened. Carmen approached the mailbox, and there it was—the thick envelope with the emblem of St. Augustine University. The rush of emotions was overwhelming, not just because of the acceptance, but because of the journey she had undergone. Just as Abraham and Sarah had seen God's promise come to fruition, so too had Carmen seen her prayers answered. She had learned to wait, to trust, to believe.

When she shared her news with her grandmother, the old woman smiled knowingly. "See? God's timing," she whispered, reminding Carmen once more of the age-old tale of faith and patience that she had read in the Bible.

Carmen nodded, realizing that the wait had offered her something more profound than an early acceptance ever could. She had discovered the strength in patience, the beauty of trust, and the timeless lesson that sometimes, the best things truly do come to those who wait in faith.

Daily Dose of Faith

* **Meditative Moments:** During moments of impatience, find a quiet spot. Sit comfortably, close your eyes, take five deep breaths, and visualize a calming scene. As you do, ask for God's reassurance and remember Abraham and Sarah's story.

* **Scriptural Solace:** Dive into stories from the Bible that highlight the importance of patience and God's timing.

* **Talk it Out:** Share your anxieties and hopes with trusted friends or mentors. Often, just verbalizing can provide clarity. Discussing biblical tales of trust can also bring peace.

* **Journal Your Journey:** Track God's workings in your life. Over time, you'll see the beautiful pattern He's weaving for you. Use stories like Sarah and Abraham as inspiration and guidance.

Living the Faith

Here's another example to consider. Djenane began gardening and soon appreciated the delicate balance of nature. Much like the biblical tale of Sarah and Abraham, her plants taught her that rushing processes often disrupts natural growth, reinforcing the beauty of patience. The waiting process mirrored the biblical lesson of Sarah and Abraham, reminding her to have faith in God's plan. This daily interaction with nature reinforced her faith in God's timing, teaching her patience and the beauty of waiting.

Journal Time!

* Recall a time when you had to wait for something crucial. How did it feel, and what was the outcome? Can you find parallels between your experience and Abraham and Sarah's wait for Isaac?

* Are there areas in your life where you're currently feeling impatient? How can the story of Sarah and Abraham provide comfort?

* How can you practice patience in daily life? Could you draw inspiration from biblical tales of perseverance?

* Write a prayer asking God for the strength to trust in His timing.

Wrapping Up the Week

Much like the changing seasons, your life has waiting periods. And as Sarah and Abraham showed, these moments of patience can lead to profound and unexpected blessings. Through stories like that of Sarah and Abraham, you are reminded that God's promises will always come to pass, even if not in the way or timing you expect. Trust in Him and His perfect plan for you.

Week 30: Learn from Mistakes

*"For though the righteous fall seven times,
they rise again."*
—Proverbs 24:16

Recommended Reading:
The story of King David (2 Samuel 11:1–5; 12:1–13)

Like everyone, even King David, known as "a man after God's own heart," had his flaws. It's not the mistakes but how you rise from them, learn, and seek redemption that defines you. His story exemplifies this journey of repentance.

You will stumble at times. It's part of being human. Like King David, your journey is marked by both highs and lows. But it's not the falling that defines you; it's how you rise, learn, and grow from your mistakes. King David, though known as "a man after God's own heart," wasn't without flaws. His story teaches you about repentance and seeking redemption.

Your True Self

As you explore and test your limits, you might err. What's important is your ability to acknowledge these missteps and work toward redemption.

Sophie's Second Chance

Sophie's desk was a meticulous arrangement of color-coded folders, to-do lists, and highlighters. With every accolade and grade that went up on her bedroom wall, there was a growing feeling of pride. She was the "go-to" person for study groups, the one friends sought for academic advice, and the teacher's favorite.

Sophie, always academically meticulous, faced an unexpected challenge with Mr. Williams's history project. Overwhelmed by her other commitments and pressed for time, she copied from her friend Rachel's assignment. But when Mr. Williams noticed, she faced the painful consequence of her action—a glaring zero.

Humiliated and adrift in a sea of regret, Sophie found herself in the school's chapel during her free period. She wasn't particularly religious, but the serenity of the space always brought her comfort. Picking up a worn-out Bible from the nearby shelf, she aimlessly flipped through its pages, landing on the story of King David.

David, the mighty king, had his fair share of imperfections. His tale was not so distant from Sophie's own, just set in a different time and context. He saw Bathsheba, wanted her, and took actions that were far from noble. Yet, when confronted by Prophet Nathan, David realized the depth of his wrongdoing. Sophie was captivated by his genuine remorse and how he sought redemption. Here was a king, a person of immense power and respect, erring, and yet finding a way back.

Inspired by David's story, Sophie grappled with her guilt. She knew she couldn't undo her actions but believed she could atone for them. Approaching Mr. Williams, she expressed her genuine remorse. Recognizing her sincerity, he gave her another chance—not for a perfect score but to understand the importance of integrity.

Sophie worked twice as hard on that assignment. And when she handed it in, she felt a sense of pride—not the kind that came from perfect scores, but from knowing she had faced her mistakes and sought to rectify them.

The incident became a turning point for Sophie. She embraced the lesson that King David's story had highlighted—that it wasn't the flawless track record that defined her, but her ability to acknowledge errors and grow from them. As years went by, Sophie often thought back to that moment, not with regret, but with gratitude for the lesson she had learned.

Life isn't about chasing perfection; it's about recognizing your imperfections, seeking redemption, and finding the resilience to rise again after setbacks.

Daily Dose of Faith

* **Forgiveness:** When you err, first ask God for forgiveness, then seek it from those you've wronged.

* **Reflection:** Spend time pondering why you made that choice. Understanding the "why" can prevent future slip-ups.

* **Accountability Partners:** Confide in a trusted friend or mentor. Sharing helps in healing and learning.

* **Scripture Guide:** Delve into Psalms, many written by David, that express remorse, seek forgiveness, and celebrate God's enduring mercy.

Living the Faith

After her mistake, Sophie not only apologized to her teacher but also led a school assembly on academic honesty. Taking inspiration from David's humility, she used her experience as a teaching moment, turning her error into a lesson for others, showcasing the power of redemption and personal growth.

Journal Time!

* Reflect on a mistake you've recently made. How did you feel afterward? What did you learn?

* How can you ensure you won't repeat similar mistakes in the future?

* How does King David's story resonate with your own experiences, and how can you use his lessons to guide your actions?

* Compose a prayer: Start by acknowledging a recent mistake, then ask God for guidance in understanding its lesson, followed by seeking strength to act with integrity in the future.

Wrapping Up the Week

While mistakes might sting initially, they often hide invaluable lessons, shaping your character and guiding your journey closer to God. They offer opportunities for growth, introspection, and drawing closer to God. King David's life teaches you that no one is above error, but with genuine repentance and a heart set on God, redemption is always within reach.

Week 31: Stay Connected to God's Love

"Neither height nor depth, nor anything else in all creation, will be able to separate us from the love of God that is in Christ Jesus our Lord."

—Romans 8:39

Recommended Reading:
The story of Hannah (1 Samuel 1:1–20)

Love is a powerful force. It binds, protects, and lifts you up. The story of Hannah showcases a profound connection between a mother and her desired child and between you and God's unwavering love. It demonstrates the depths of longing and the powerful faith one might hold when grounded in that divine connection.

In her deep anguish due to her childlessness and the ridicule she faced, Hannah's fervent prayers and vow to God showcased her profound relationship with Him. Her unyielding faith, even when faced with despair and societal pressure, underscores the strength of her bond with the Divine. When she was blessed with Samuel and later dedicated him to the Lord's service, her actions became a testament to her unwavering faith and deep connection with God's love and purpose for her.

Your True Self

In today's fast-paced world, with numerous distractions, pressures, and fleeting relationships, the challenge is staying anchored despite the chaos; it's easy to feel lost and disconnected. This disconnection might make you wonder if there's a bond as deep and unwavering as Hannah's in your life. Hannah's story reminds you of the depth and steadfastness of God's love—a bond that remains unbroken regardless of your circumstances.

Whispers in the Wind

As Esfir grew older, she cherished the quiet moments spent with her grandmother, Nana Halene. They often found solace in the garden, where Nana Halene would share stories of her youth. Amid these tales, Esfir was captivated by one particular story that Nana Halene held close to her heart—the story of her childhood friend, Isabella.

"Isabella and I were inseparable as children," Nana Halene began, her eyes clouding with the mist of long-past memories. "But as the years passed and we stepped into womanhood, a painful realization cast a shadow over Isabella's life: she couldn't bear children. The weight of this reality bore heavily on her, much like Hannah in the scriptures."

As Nana Halene mentioned Hannah from the scriptures, Esfir's memory from her Sunday school lessons sprang to the forefront, and she nodded in understanding. She remembered the biblical tale of Hannah, a woman who prayed fervently to God for a child, promising to dedicate her son to the Lord's service.

Nana Halene continued, "While most saw Isabella's barrenness as a closed chapter, she saw it as a blank page waiting to be written. Her faith was unwavering. Every evening, I'd see her at the garden's edge, her lips moving in silent prayer, her face bathed in the golden hue of sunset. Her resilience reminded me of Hannah's story."

Esfir's eyes widened, "Did her prayers get answered?"

Nana Halene smiled. "One evening, with a mysterious twinkle in her eye, Isabella invited me to her home, saying she had a surprise. There, wrapped in a blanket, was a tiny baby with eyes as bright as the stars. She had adopted a child, abandoned by her family. Isabella believed that her prayers had been answered, but not in the way she'd expected. Instead of giving birth, she was chosen to give a mother's love."

Esfir felt a lump in her throat, deeply moved by the story. "So, in a way, her faith was rewarded, just like Hannah's?"

"In its own special way," Nana Halene replied. "Both Isabella and Hannah taught me that faith isn't about receiving exactly what we ask for, but about being open to the unexpected ways God answers our prayers."

As the years passed, Esfir faced her own challenges, like when she lost her job unexpectedly. In those moments of despair, the story of Isabella and the biblical tale of Hannah reminded her of the power of unwavering faith. When faced with challenges, she remembered Isabella's story and the biblical tale of Hannah, drawing strength from their unwavering faith.

Years later, Esfir found herself narrating the same story to her daughter. "Remember," she'd conclude, "faith doesn't always move in the direction we expect. It dances and swirls, changing its rhythm with the challenges we face. And sometimes, even when it seems like it's taking a step back, it's only preparing to leap forward. But if you listen closely, you'll hear its whispers in the wind, guiding you, just like it did for Isabella and Hannah."

Daily Dose of Faith

* **Daily Prayer:** Begin and end your day with a prayer to feel God's love and guidance. Let it remind you of the same dedication and love Hannah felt for God.

- **Community:** Engage in group prayers or youth Bible study groups to foster connections rooted in faith.

- **Acts of Kindness:** Show God's love through small acts of kindness, mirroring Hannah's dedication. Every act of love echoes Hannah's unwavering commitment to God.

- **Scriptural Reflection:** Dive into verses about God's love, such as Romans 8:38–39, to understand its magnitude.

Living the Faith

Here's another example to consider. Lissette started visiting her grandmother regularly, reading Bible verses to her, and praying by her bedside. Through these actions, Lissette felt a deeper connection, not just with her family, but with God. Her dedication was a testament to God's love manifesting through human bonds. This mirrored Hannah's unwavering dedication to God, further showing how biblical tales can resonate in your own life.

Journal Time!

- Reflect on a relationship in your life that showcases deep love and loyalty. What makes it special?

- How can you mirror Hannah's dedication in your everyday life? Can you find moments that remind you of the unyielding bond between Hannah and God?

- How do you stay connected to God's love during challenging times?

- Write a prayer asking God to strengthen your bonds with Him and with those around you, helping you to embody His love daily.

Wrapping Up the Week

The bonds of love and faith can light your way even in the darkest times. While the world can sometimes feel cold and isolating, stories like that of Hannah remind you of the warmth and strength you can find in those bonds. In a way, you have a Hannah story within you. As you navigate life's challenges, strive to emulate Hannah's dedication and remain anchored in God's unwavering love.

Week 32: Embrace Change

*"Therefore, if anyone is in Christ, the new creation has
come: The old has gone, the new is here!"*
—2 Corinthians 5:17

Recommended Reading:
**The story of the Israelites' escape from Egypt
(Exodus 14:10–22)**

Life is a series of changes, from small daily shifts to significant life events.
Change can be both invigorating and daunting. The story of the Israelites
in Exodus gives you insights into navigating change with faith and hope,
reminding you that every transition has a purpose.

The Israelites, once enslaved in Egypt under Pharaoh's rule, were led
by Moses through the Red Sea and into the wilderness on their way to
the Promised Land after Pharaoh finally relented to let them go. Their
journey was filled with challenges, doubts, miracles, and lessons. From
the splitting of the Red Sea to receiving manna from heaven, they
experienced God's providence and learned to rely on Him in times
of change.

Your True Self

You face an ever-changing world, from navigating the complexities of
social media, adjusting to new educational formats like online
schooling, to evolving relationships, and personal growth.

While it's tempting to resist or fear change, embracing it can lead to unexpected blessings and growth. The Israelites' journey from bondage to freedom can inspire you to see change not as an end, but as a new beginning.

Allison's Exodus

The walls of Allison's bedroom were stripped of their colorful posters and cherished memories, revealing plain white underneath. A sentiment of emptiness lingered, contrasting sharply with the once lively space. Each packed box felt like a piece of her past being sealed away. A familiar life of school dances, cherished friendships, and neighborhood games was coming to an end.

She had often complained about the monotony of life in her small town. But now that she was leaving, all she yearned for was one more ordinary day in it.

As she taped up the last box, her younger brother, Ben, entered, clutching his worn-out teddy bear. "Allie, will our new place have the same stars?" he asked, his voice laden with a touch of vulnerability.

She smiled, hugging him close. "Yes, buddy, the same stars, moon, and sun."

That night, as she lay on her mattress—her bed already disassembled— her mind wandered to a story her grandma once narrated. The story of the Israelites and their Exodus. A tale of a community uprooting themselves from the known, journeying across deserts, facing hardships, but moving with hope toward a land of promise.

Closing her eyes, Allison tried to harness some of their courage. Their journey was filled with monumental challenges, but it also depicted growth, discovery, and profound faith. "Can I find that faith within me?" she whispered into the stillness.

The next morning dawned with the blaring of the moving truck's horn. The family got into motion, bustling around, ensuring everything was packed. Allison, however, took a moment. She walked to her favorite spot, the oak tree in her backyard. She had spent countless hours perched on its branches, weaving dreams.

As she touched the tree bark, she felt an unexpected sense of grounding. "Just as the Israelites moved from a place of bondage to freedom, life is not static," she thought. "And neither am I." The tree, too, had grown from a sapling to this grand stature, enduring storms and sunshine alike. It had changed, and so would she.

The journey to the new city felt like a voyage through time. Fields and towns passed by her window, a shifting landscape symbolizing the transition she was undergoing. Allison found herself reflecting on the Israelites' endurance and unwavering spirit. "Maybe this move is my desert," she mused, "a space where I rediscover and reinvent."

Arrival at their new home was met with a mixture of exhaustion and anticipation. It was a beautiful house, set against a backdrop of rolling hills. The neighbors, having heard of their arrival, came over with homemade pies and welcoming smiles.

Days turned into weeks, and the unfamiliar began to morph into the known. Allison joined a new school, made friends, and even discovered a passion for photography, capturing her new surroundings' beauty. Ben, too, quickly adjusted, often reminding her of the constellations they both recognized.

One evening, as Allison sat on the porch, she realized the trepidation she once felt had evolved into a profound sense of gratitude. She had navigated her personal exodus, embraced change, and in the process, discovered newer facets of herself.

And as the same stars shone down on her, Allison felt deeply connected—to her past, her present, and the infinite possibilities of her future, understanding that just as the Israelites found promise after change, so could she.

Daily Dose of Faith

* **Morning Reflection:** Start your day by acknowledging one change you're grateful for.

* **Seek Guidance:** When faced with challenging transitions, pray for God's wisdom and direction. Consider reciting Psalms 32:8, "I will instruct you and teach you in the way you should go; I will counsel you with my eye upon you."

* **Stay Adaptable:** Embrace flexibility in daily life, practicing patience and resilience.

* **Connect with Stories:** Read about the journeys of biblical figures who faced and overcame change with God's help.

Living the Faith

Here's another example to consider. Allison made an effort to find a youth group in her new town, connecting with peers who shared her faith. In the stories they shared, she could see echoes of the Israelites' perseverance and faith. They welcomed her, shared their own stories of change, and soon, Allison realized that change wasn't something to fear but an opportunity to grow in her faith and as an individual.

Journal Time!

* What changes are you currently facing? How do you feel about them?

* Recall a past change in your life. How did it shape you?

* How can the story of the Israelites inspire you to approach change differently?

* Write a prayer asking God to guide you through times of transition and to strengthen your faith.

Wrapping Up the Week

Just as a river's course changes over time, carving new paths and landscapes, you too, like the Israelites, embark on journeys of change. By leaning into your faith and trusting in God's plan, you can navigate these shifts with grace and optimism, understanding that each transition is an opportunity to grow closer to Him and your true purpose. The same faith that guided the Israelites can light your path, showing you the blessings inherent in every change. Embrace change with an open heart and see the wonders it can bring.

Week 33: Lean on God in Times of Need

"Cast all your anxiety on him because he cares for you."
—1 Peter 5:7

> **Recommended Reading:**
> The story of the Widow of Zarephath (1 Kings 17:7–24)

Life has a way of presenting challenges that can make you feel desolate and overwhelmed. Much like the Widow of Zarephath faced desperation during a time of famine, you too might encounter moments of despair in the throes of life's challenges. During these times, remember to lean on God, just as the widow did. This week, you'll explore how God is ever-present, especially during your times of need.

In 1 Kings 17, the Widow of Zarephath was on the brink of using her last bit of food for herself and her son, expecting them to die afterward. Her journey, brimming with scarcity and later abundance, mirrors the ups and downs you might experience in life. Yet, through the prophet Elijah, God ensured that her jar of flour did not run out and her jug of oil did not run dry. This story illustrates that God's providence often comes in miraculous ways during your times of need.

Your True Self

From school stresses, friendship challenges, to personal struggles, you face a plethora of pressures. These challenges aren't so different from what the Widow of Zarephath faced—feelings of despair, isolation, and hopelessness. But there's a constant source of strength and solace: God. The widow's experience reminds you that, even in moments of profound despair, God's comforting presence is just a prayer away.

The Quiet Call of Faith

The pale-blue envelope bore the insignia of Tara's dream university. Just as the Widow of Zarephath faced the dire prospect of starvation during a famine, Tara confronted despair after her long journey of preparation. The weight of the paper felt strangely heavy as she slid her finger under the seal. Skimming through the letter, her heart sank. "We regret to inform you..."

Tears blurred her vision as she tossed the letter onto her desk. Much like the desperation the Widow of Zarephath felt, Tara's once comforting room now seemed cold and distant. Posters of campus life, academic brochures, and scholarship applications seemed to mock her. All her meticulous plans, late-night study sessions, and sacrifices felt in vain.

Seeking comfort, she reached for her grandmother's old Bible, turning to the story of the Widow of Zarephath—a tale she often found solace in. The stories within had always been a source of guidance during her difficult times. The widow's trust in God, even in the face of extreme adversity, was inspiring. Tara felt a resonance with the widow's trust and reliance on God.

Feeling a renewed sense of calm, Tara decided to seek advice and support. Like the widow, who trusted in the prophet Elijah's words, Tara too reached out to her mentor, Ms. Jensen, and discovered new opportunities.

Daily Dose of Faith

* **Reach Out:** When feeling down, pray. Share your feelings and worries with God.

* **Seek Support:** Connect with a trusted friend or mentor to talk about what you're going through.

* **Scripture Solace:** Dive into verses that remind you of God's steadfast love and support.

* **Pause and Reflect:** Take a moment each day to find a quiet space and meditate on God's presence.

Living the Faith

Reflecting upon the story of the Widow of Zarephath, Tara found renewed hope and direction. Just as the widow's faith led to miracles, Tara too felt directed to a new path after her setback. She joined a youth group and felt inspired by the connections she made. The story of the widow became her anchor.

Journal Time!

* Have you ever felt overwhelmed, like the Widow of Zarephath? Describe that.

* In what subtle ways has God shown His presence in your life?

* What challenges are you facing right now? How can you lean on God during these times?

* Write a prayer, asking God for strength, guidance, and the ability to recognize His whispers in your life.

Wrapping Up the Week

While you'll face challenges, with God's guidance, you'll never be alone. The stories of both the Widow of Zarephath and Tara serve as testimonials. Remember that during your most trying moments, if you lean on God and stay open-hearted, you can witness His miraculous ways. Turn to Him, for He is your refuge and strength.

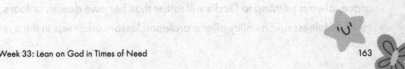

Week 34: Pursue a Life of Humility

"For all those who exalt themselves will be humbled,
and those who humble themselves will be exalted."
—Luke 14:11

Recommended Reading:
The Annunciation to Mary (Luke 1:26–38)

Society often celebrates those who stand out and assert themselves, but there's an enduring strength found in the quietness of humility. This week, immerse yourself in the story of Mary, a young woman whose humility set the stage for the arrival of the Savior.

In the Book of Luke, the angel Gabriel visits Mary, a young woman betrothed to Joseph. The angel delivers the news that she would conceive the Son of God. Mary's response is telling of her character: "Behold, I am the servant of the Lord; let it be to me according to your word." Despite the enormity of this revelation, Mary's humility shines brightly. She doesn't seek fame or recognition but humbly accepts the role that God has chosen for her.

Being the mother of the Messiah was no small responsibility, fraught with challenges, scrutiny, and sacrifice. Yet, Mary embraced this role with grace, always pointing to God's will rather than her own desires or fears. Her faithfulness and humility offer a profound lesson: greatness in the eyes of God is not about our achievements or status but our willingness to serve Him with a humble heart.

Your True Self

Much like Mary, who was entrusted with a great task yet remained humble, you are called to embrace your achievements without letting them define your self-worth. In an age of social media and the constant push to "show off" achievements, maintaining humility can be a challenge. Still, as you navigate these pressures, understanding true humility can be the difference between a life of fulfillment and one of emptiness. True humility is about recognizing your strengths and achievements without overshadowing others. After all, these talents and successes come from God.

A Light in Humility

In the bustling hallways of Jericho High, where accomplishments were the currency of reputation, Jasmine stood apart. Not because her list of accolades was the longest, though it undoubtedly was, but because of the gentle humility with which she wore her successes.

Her peers often whispered, "How does she manage it all?" Jasmine was a marvel in the classroom, a force on the soccer field, and a sensation in the school's annual art show. Yet, unlike others who'd reached similar heights, Jasmine never reveled in the spotlight. In a manner akin to Mary, she believed in letting her achievements speak for themselves.

It wasn't a coincidence that her favorite historical figure was Mary, the mother of Jesus, who, despite being chosen to bear the Savior of mankind, remained grounded in her humility and devotion to God. Her mother had introduced her to Mary's story when she was younger, and Jasmine took to heart the lesson that true greatness is derived from humble acceptance of God's will.

One chilly November morning, as students pored over their textbooks in the school library, Jane, a girl from Jasmine's class, hesitated by her table. Jane was bright and vivacious but math, particularly algebra, was her Achilles' heel.

Swallowing her apprehension, Jane mustered up the courage to ask, "Jasmine, could you help me with this problem?"

Jasmine looked up, her eyes warm. "Of course, have a seat."

Over the next few weeks, the library's corner table became a regular meeting spot for the two. Emulating the humble teachings of Mary, Jasmine used her strengths to uplift others, not to belittle them. With her gift for numbers and immense patience, Jasmine would guide Jane through equations and problems, breaking them down in ways that Jane could grasp.

What was special about these sessions wasn't just the transfer of knowledge. It was the way Jasmine taught. She never flaunted her expertise, never sighed in exasperation, and most importantly, never made Jane feel inferior. When Jane would get frustrated or overwhelmed, Jasmine would reassure her with anecdotes of her own struggles, sharing stories of times she faced challenges and how she overcame them.

Word spread of Jasmine's kindness. Soon, their duo expanded, with more students joining the impromptu tutoring sessions. Thanks to Jasmine's welcoming spirit, a community of learners formed, replacing the hierarchy.

One evening, as they were wrapping up, Jane, with teary eyes, handed Jasmine a hand-painted card. On it was a depiction of Mary, holding baby Jesus, with the words, "To the one who leads with humility."

Jasmine looked up, surprised and touched. "This is beautiful, Jane. Thank you."

Jane smiled, "You've done more for me than just help with math. Like Mary, you've led with a humility that's rare and inspiring. You've shown me that true greatness is in lifting others."

The year progressed, and while Jasmine continued to excel, it wasn't her medals or certificates that made her memorable. It was her kindness, her humility, and the way she made everyone feel valued.

In the graduation yearbook, the editors chose a quote for Jasmine's photo instead of listing her many accolades: "Success is not in being the best, but in bringing out the best in others."

And for anyone who knew Jasmine, that sentiment captured her essence perfectly.

Daily Dose of Faith

* **Self-Reflection:** Spend a few minutes daily recognizing your blessings and giving thanks to God.

* **Lift Others:** Compliment someone genuinely every day, focusing on their strengths.

* **Seek Guidance:** Reflect on Mary's life and see how you can incorporate her humility into your own journey.

* **Serve:** Find a way to help someone in need, without expecting anything in return.

Living the Faith

Jasmine's humility became infectious. Others started recognizing their blessings without overshadowing their peers. The school environment shifted, becoming one where students celebrated each other's successes without jealousy, channeling the spirit of Mary and her humble acceptance of God's will.

Journal Time!

* Think of a situation where you showcased humility. How did it make you feel?

* How do you feel when you encounter someone humble versus someone arrogant?

* Consider Mary's journey. How does it inspire you to live with humility in today's world?

* Write a prayer asking God to help you walk the path of humility, just like Mary did.

Wrapping Up the Week

True leadership emanates from the grace of quiet humility, not from the volume of one's voice. Mary, chosen to be the mother of the Savior, showcased that by leading with a gentle spirit and a humble heart. In a world that often shouts, learn to whisper, for within those whispers lies the profound strength of humility. Let the life of Mary guide you, reminding you that humility is not a sign of weakness but of true strength.

Week 35: Cultivate a Heart of Compassion

"Be kind and compassionate to one another, forgiving each other, just as in Christ God forgave you."
—Ephesians 4:32

Recommended Reading:
The story of Jesus healing the leper (Mark 1:40–45)

In your daily interactions, even the smallest act of compassion can have a transformative impact on someone's life. This week, you'll focus on the profound act of Jesus healing the leper, highlighting the boundless compassion that Jesus exemplified.

In Mark 1:40–45, a man with leprosy approached Jesus, hoping for healing. In those times, lepers were shunned, considered unclean. But Jesus, moved with compassion, reached out and touched the man, saying, "Be clean." Instantly, the leprosy disappeared. This wasn't just a miracle of healing, but a powerful demonstration of Jesus's compassionate heart.

Your True Self

Life can be overwhelming. With academic pressures, social expectations, and the quest for self-identity, it's easy to become self-centered. True growth and happiness arise when you show compassion, as Jesus did, especially to those often overlooked by society.

Megan's Gift

On a frigid winter morning, snowflakes fluttered down, blanketing the streets in white. As students hurried into Jericho High, shielded by coats and scarves, a lone figure sat huddled by the school's entrance. An elderly woman, her fingers blue with cold, her eyes dull with despair.

Many students hurried by, lost in the excitement of the upcoming holidays, exams, or the latest gossip. But Megan, remembering Jesus's act of compassion toward the ostracized leper, couldn't just walk past. She paused. A memory from Sunday school flashed through her mind—the story of Jesus and the leper, an outcast whom everyone avoided, but whom Jesus approached with compassion.

Tentatively, she walked over to the woman. Up close, Megan could see the lines of hardship etched on her face, the tremble of her cold hands, and the slow rhythm of her shivering breaths.

"Hi there," Megan began gently, "It's really cold today. Would you like my gloves?"

The woman looked up, surprise evident in her watery eyes. "Oh, dear, you need them too."

Megan smiled, her heart warming despite the chill. "I have another pair at home. Please, take these." She handed over her thick, woolen gloves, watching as the woman slipped them on, her fingers sighing in relief.

Recalling how Jesus showed compassion to the leper, Megan understood the power of simple acts to profoundly affect someone's life. Feeling emboldened, Megan took out the sandwich she'd packed for lunch. "I thought you might be hungry," she said, handing it over. The woman's gratitude was palpable, her voice choked as she whispered, "Thank you."

But Megan didn't just leave after her gifts. She sat down beside the woman, brushing snow off a spot. They talked. The woman introduced herself as Mrs. Thompson. She spoke of better days, of a family she once had, and of the string of misfortunes that led her to the streets.

And Megan? She listened. Truly listened, just as Jesus had listened and responded to the pleas of the leper, with an empathy and understanding that belied her young age. Mrs. Thompson's stories weren't just tales of a homeless woman; they were the life chapters of someone who'd once been a mother, a wife, a friend.

Word spread throughout the day about Megan's compassionate gesture. By afternoon, a group of students, led by Megan, started a mini drive, collecting blankets, clothes, and some food for Mrs. Thompson and others like her.

Mrs. Thompson's presence outside the school was short-lived. A local shelter, alerted by the school administration, came to assist her. But the impression she left on Megan, and the ripple effect of kindness she inspired in the student community, lingered much longer.

A few months later, in spring, the school planted a tree in its yard. Named "The Compassion Tree," it stood as a lasting symbol of kindness, a reminder that compassion can take root and flourish in the unlikeliest of places. It served as a living reminder of that cold winter day when a young girl, inspired by a biblical act of kindness, reached out to a stranger, showing her school and her community that sometimes, just as Jesus demonstrated, the warmth of a kind heart can outshine the coldest of days.

Daily Dose of Faith

* **Mindful Moments:** Start your day by reflecting on one act of compassion you can carry out.

* **Active Listening:** When someone speaks, give them your full attention. It's a simple yet powerful act of compassion.

* **Volunteer:** Dedicate some time each month to a cause close to your heart.

* **Spread Kindness:** Compliment or encourage someone daily. Your words might be the support they need.

Living the Faith

Moved by Megan's kindness and drawing inspiration from Jesus's teachings, several students founded a compassion club. Its mission? To spread love and kindness within the school community, embodying the biblical lessons of caring for one another. From arranging clothing drives to volunteering at shelters, they actively spread love, showing that the ripple effect of one compassionate act can create a wave of kindness.

Journal Time!

* Recall a moment when someone showed you unexpected compassion. How did it make you feel?

* What's a situation where you felt the need to show compassion but hesitated? What held you back?

* Reflect on ways you can integrate compassion into your daily life.

* Write a prayer, asking God to fill your heart with the same compassion Jesus embodied.

Wrapping Up the Week

Compassion isn't measured by grand gestures alone; it's often found in everyday moments, in listening, in understanding, and in reaching out. It's about seeing the unseen, touching the untouched, just as Jesus did with the leper. It's in the simple acts—a listening ear, a comforting word, a helpful hand. Jesus showcased the profound impact of compassion, teaching you that when you touch lives with kindness, you reflect the love of God in the purest way.

Week 36: Strengthen Your Faith Community

"And let us consider how we may spur one another on toward love and good deeds, not giving up meeting together, as some are in the habit of doing, but encouraging one another—and all the more as you see the Day approaching."

—Hebrews 10:24–25

Recommended Reading:
The story of Gideon (Judges 6)

Community is the foundation of your faith journey. It's where you find support, learn, and grow. Much like the community that supported Gideon, Gideon's story serves as a testament to the strength and success achievable when a community comes together in faith.

In Judges 6, the Israelites were suffering, living under the harsh rule of the Midianites. God chose Gideon, an unlikely leader, to deliver His people. Despite his doubts, with God's guidance and the support of his community, Gideon managed to rally the Israelites. Together, with faith and unity, they overcame the mighty Midianite army against all odds.

Your True Self

In today's world, with platforms like social media often highlighting individual achievements over collective efforts, it can be easy to overlook the power of community. But remember, just as Gideon and the Israelites demonstrated, while personal faith is essential, the collective faith of a community can move mountains.

Lily's Legacy

Lily entered the basement of her church, a large dimly lit space that served as the youth group's gathering spot. Gideon's tale of unity and strength had inspired Lily, and she'd joined the youth group a year ago, seeking connection and community. But even among fellow members, she sometimes felt like an outsider looking in. The group was diverse; athletes sat with athletes, artists with artists, and scholars formed their own clusters. They rarely mingled beyond their comfort zones.

One evening, while reading the story of Gideon in her room, Lily had an epiphany. She realized that just as Gideon united the Israelites, perhaps the youth group needed a joint mission, something to unify them and emphasize their collective strength.

The next week, with the permission of the church leaders, Lily proposed a project: to transform the basement into a vibrant community space. But there was a twist. Each member would draw lots, and they'd be paired with someone from a different clique. Together, they'd take on a specific task for the renovation. She hoped to channel the same unity and faith Gideon inspired in his people.

At first, the idea was met with skepticism. Some thought it was too ambitious; others were hesitant about the idea of working outside their comfort zones. But Lily's conviction won them over.

Over the next two months, the basement buzzed with activity. The athletes, with their physical strength, took on heavy lifting and carpentry. The artists brainstormed murals and design elements. The scholars documented the transformation process, planning to create a digital chronicle of their journey.

Lily watched with joy as barriers broke down. She saw Jake, the star quarterback, laughing as he painted walls with Clara, the introverted poet. Sophie, the debate team captain, was deep in conversation with Mark, the drummer from the church band, discussing the best way to set up the new sound system.

On the day of the final reveal, the basement was transformed. The walls were adorned with murals, the seating was cohesive and welcoming, and the ambiance radiated warmth. But more than the physical changes, the atmosphere had shifted. The once distinct clusters of youth now mingled freely, their conversations echoing the newfound unity.

The church leaders were astounded, not just by the renovated space, but by the palpable change in the group's dynamics. They'd become more cohesive, more attuned to one another's strengths and weaknesses.

Lily, looking around the transformed space, felt a deep sense of accomplishment. This wasn't just about a renovated basement; it was about the power of unity and faith. It was a modern reflection of Gideon's story.

In the years that followed, the basement wasn't just a gathering spot for the youth. It became a testament to the power of unity and faith, reminiscent of Gideon's story.

Daily Dose of Faith

* **Group Study:** Dive deep into stories like Gideon's, and organize weekly Bible study sessions with friends or members of your church.

- * **Community Service:** Strengthen your faith community by serving the larger community around you.

- * **Prayer Circles:** Host regular prayer meetings, emphasizing the needs and challenges within your community.

- * **Share Stories:** Encourage sharing personal faith journeys within your group. This builds understanding and connection.

Living the Faith

After their successful project, Lily's group began monthly initiatives that combined faith lessons with community service. Their bonds strengthened, and soon, inspired by Gideon's example, they became an exemplary model for other youth groups, showing the potential of a united faith community.

Journal Time!

- * Think of a time when unity within your community or group helped overcome a significant challenge. How does it relate to Gideon's story?

- * Reflect on the strengths of your faith community. What can be improved?

- * Write a prayer for the unity and strength of your faith community, asking for the same faith and unity Gideon and the Israelites displayed.

Wrapping Up the Week

We all need each other, especially on our faith journey. Gideon's leadership and the unity of his community teach you that with trust in God and unity in community, challenges can be surmounted. In our world today, strive to build, nurture, and lean on our faith communities. Together, as a united faith community, we can illuminate even the darkest moments with hope and strength.

Week 37: Be a Good Steward

*"Moreover, it is required of stewards
that they be found faithful."*
—1 Corinthians 4:2

Recommended Reading:
The parable of the talents (Matthew 25:14–30)

God has blessed you with gifts and resources. In the parable of the talents (Matthew 25:14–30), you are called to be an active steward; the Bible emphasizes the importance of not just preserving but also multiplying and effectively using these gifts. Being a good steward isn't about hoarding; it's about purposeful and beneficial utilization.

In the parable, a master entrusts his servants with varying amounts of money. Two of them invest and double their money, while the third hides his in the ground. The master praises the first two for their diligence and foresight but reprimands the third for his fear and inaction. This narrative challenges you to ask: are you maximizing the gifts and resources God has given you, or are you burying them out of fear? This story emphasizes the significance of wisely using the resources you're given.

Your True Self

In a society that often emphasizes consumption over conservation, you face the pressure to constantly acquire more. But as the parable suggests, it's not about how much you have, but how you use it. However, true

178

value doesn't lie in the abundance of possessions but in how you manage and utilize what you have.

Enzokuhle's Jar System

Every Saturday morning, Enzokuhle's father handed her a crisp twenty-dollar bill, her weekly allowance. For most kids her age, this would be an immediate ticket to a treat, toy, or game. But Enzokuhle had a system, a method that embodied the spirit of the parable—multiplying her resources responsibly, inspired by a lesson she learned from her grandmother about stewardship and the power of intentional spending.

On the shelf in her room stood three clear jars labeled: Save, Give, and Spend. The idea was simple but profound. Just like the servants entrusted with talents, Enzokuhle was accountable for her "talents"—in this case, her allowance. Whenever she received her allowance or any other money, she'd divide it amongst the jars.

Ten dollars went straight into the Save jar, representing her commitment to her future. Five dollars went into Give, which she'd set aside to help those less fortunate. The remaining five went to Spend, allowing her some immediate joy without guilt.

As weeks turned into months, Enzokuhle began noticing the weight in her Save jar increasing. She'd often shake it, the sound of accumulating coins serving as a melodic reminder of her diligence. She wasn't saving for anything specific; it was more about understanding the value of money and realizing she didn't need to spend instantly.

Her Give jar was a different kind of fulfillment. At the end of each month, she'd count out the money and choose a local charity to donate to. Sometimes it was the animal shelter, other times the community food bank, and occasionally, a global charity. Her consistent contributions might have seemed small, but over time, they began making tangible impacts. One month, her donation helped buy new blankets for the shelter, and another time, it sponsored a school kit for a child overseas. Receiving thank-you letters and seeing the results of her contributions, Enzokuhle realized the power of consistent giving, no matter how small.

The Spend jar, though it had the least, brought her immediate pleasure. She'd sometimes buy a book, get an ice cream, or save for a few weeks to get something slightly bigger. The limited funds in this jar taught her to think about her purchases and prioritize what truly mattered.

One day, her school announced a field trip that had a fee attached. Some of Enzokuhle's classmates fretted about the cost. Enzokuhle paused, considering her choices, and then, with confidence, went to her Save jar. She had acted wisely with her resources, just like the diligent servants in the parable. She felt a swell of pride realizing she had more than enough to cover the trip and even offered to help a friend who was short on funds.

The jars were more than just containers for her money; they became symbols of her values. In a way, each jar was a reflection of the talents from the parable—some were multiplied, some were generously shared, and some were prudently spent. Word spread about Enzokuhle's system, and soon some of her friends adopted similar methods, adapting it to fit their individual needs.

By the end of the year, not only had Enzokuhle accumulated a nice sum in her savings, but she'd also contributed significantly to causes she cared about and made thoughtful purchases without ever feeling deprived.

As she looked at the three jars on her shelf, she realized they weren't just about money management. They were life lessons in patience, compassion, and prudence. Each jar, each coin, served as a daily reminder: stewardship wasn't solely about managing money, but about shaping one's approach to life itself.

Daily Dose of Faith

* **Budgeting:** Learn to manage your finances wisely. Allocate parts for saving, giving, and spending.

* **Talent Time:** Dedicate some time each week to hone a skill or talent God has blessed you with.

* **Share and Care:** Offer your skills or knowledge to help someone else, perhaps by tutoring, mentoring, or volunteering.

* **Respect Resources:** Whether it's time, money, or the environment, show gratitude by being responsible.

Living the Faith

Inspired by the parable, Enzokuhle started a club at her school where students exchanged skills, teaching and learning from each other. By sharing and developing their talents, they lived out the essence of the parable, ensuring none of their gifts were buried or wasted. This not only enhanced their talents but also strengthened their sense of community and stewardship.

Journal Time!

* List the talents or resources God has blessed you with. How are you currently using them?

* Reflect on a moment when you felt proud of how you managed a particular gift or resource.

* Are there areas in your life where you could be a better steward?

* Write a personal commitment on how you plan to be more responsible with your gifts moving forward.

Wrapping Up the Week

As you embrace the lessons from the parable of the talents and Enzokuhle's story, you might see that stewardship is a comprehensive principle, touching every aspect of our lives. It's about recognizing God's gifts, whether they're talents, time, or treasures, and using them wisely for our growth and the betterment of our communities. In living out this principle of stewardship, you'll not only grow personally but also reflect the lessons from the parable of the talents. In embracing stewardship, you honor God and the trust He places in you.

Week 38: Let Go of Control

"In their hearts humans plan their course,
but the Lord establishes their steps."
—Proverbs 16:9

Recommended Reading:
The story of Jonah running from God's call (Jonah 1:1–3)

Life doesn't always go as you envision, and sometimes your plans differ from God's. Just as Jonah had to relinquish his control and follow God's direction, the challenge is not in planning, but in surrendering control when the need arises and trusting in His divine guidance.

Jonah, when called by God to prophesy in Nineveh, chose to run away. His escape led him into the belly of a big fish. After three days, he was spat out, having realized he couldn't outrun God's plan. Eventually, he went to Nineveh, conveying God's message. Jonah's story reminds you that God's plan, even if challenging or unexpected, always has purpose.

Your True Self

The world around you often tells you that to be in control is to be powerful. However, as Jonah's tale illustrates, true power and understanding come when you let go and trust in God's plan. Yet, there's a unique strength in vulnerability, in admitting that you don't have all the answers and in letting God take the lead. This balance between control and surrender is a journey of self-discovery.

Alyssa's Time Capsule

Alyssa's life was a carefully constructed jigsaw puzzle, each piece meticulously placed to fit into the next. Like Jonah, who initially wanted control over his destiny, she too wanted a grasp on every moment of her life. Her schedule was no exception: a color-coded, hour-by-hour roadmap on her planner. Red for school, blue for extracurriculars, green for personal time, and purple for rest. She found comfort in knowing what each moment held, until life decided to shake things up.

One Tuesday, a day etched in Alyssa's mind, everything unraveled. It was as if she was thrown into the belly of a big fish, much like Jonah, facing the unpredictability of life head-on. Her day, her week, her whole balance felt thrown off.

Anxiety, like a shadow, crept in. How was she to reshuffle, to fit everything back, to maintain her high standards? She tried to reorganize, but the more she attempted to control, the more the pieces seemed to scatter.

Seeing her daughter's distress, Alyssa's godmother gently intervened one evening. "Life" she began, "isn't a series of boxes to be checked off. It's more like a river, continuously flowing, changing course, sometimes unpredictable but always moving forward."

She took Alyssa to their attic, where they unearthed an old family treasure: a hand-woven blanket made by Alyssa's great-grandmother. "She wove this without a clear design in mind," her godmother explained. "Just adding patterns and colors as she felt. There were mistakes, tangled threads, and uneven patches. But look how beautiful it is as a whole."

Alyssa realized her life didn't always have to be planned to the minute. Jonah's journey in the belly of the fish gave him time to reflect and understand God's plan. Similarly, these disruptions gave Alyssa the chance to reflect on the essence of life and the need to sometimes let go.

Taking a deep breath, she began to practice letting go. She started small, allowing herself breaks when she felt like it, not just when her planner said she could. She accepted changes without trying to resist them, recognizing that some events were simply out of her control.

With time, Alyssa's perspective transformed. She started valuing spontaneity, finding joy in unexpected meetups with friends, last-minute plans, or simply lounging with a book when she felt like it. The need to control every moment waned, replaced by a more profound understanding of life's ebb and flow.

Months later, when her tennis coach praised her improved performance, she smiled. It wasn't additional practice; it was the newfound flexibility in her mindset. Instead of being rigid and tense, trying to stick to a plan, she became adaptive, responding to the ball as it came.

Alyssa's meticulously color-coded planner still existed, but now, blank spaces peppered its pages, representing unplanned moments and spontaneous joys. These white gaps were no longer sources of anxiety; they were symbols of freedom.

By learning to trust the process, Alyssa discovered a greater truth: Just as Jonah found purpose in Nineveh after he surrendered to God's plan, she found that life's beauty wasn't always in the precision of planned moments, but often in the serendipity of the unplanned.

Daily Dose of Faith

* **Prayerful Pause:** Begin each morning with a prayer, surrendering your plans to God and being open to His direction.

* **Reflective Journaling:** Note down moments when you felt the urge to control and how it made you feel. Over time, you might recognize patterns and learn healthier coping mechanisms.

* **Release Ritual:** When overwhelmed, write down your worries and fears on a piece of paper, and then safely burn or bury it as a symbolic act of letting go.

Living the Faith

Alyssa started practicing "Surrender Sundays," where she let go of her meticulous planning for one day, a nod to Jonah's realization of surrendering to God's will. She soon found that these were her most refreshing and spontaneous days, filled with unexpected joys.

Journal Time!

* Think about a time you tried to control an outcome. What were the results? How did it make you feel?

* Reflect on moments you've seen God's hand in your life, guiding you in unexpected ways.

* Write a prayer asking God to help you surrender control and trust in His divine guidance.

* Are there areas in your life where you find it especially hard to let go? Why do you think that is?

Wrapping Up the Week

Control can offer comfort, like a familiar room, but if you're not careful, that room can become a cage. Much like Jonah found peace and purpose after letting go of his initial resistance, true freedom and growth often lie in surrendering, in trusting God's plan, and in understanding that His vision for you may lead to unexpected, yet beautiful destinations.

Week 39: Walk in Obedience

"If you love me, you will keep my commandments."
—John 14:15

Recommended Reading:
The story of Abraham in the Book of Genesis
(Genesis 12:1–4)

Obedience often requires sacrifice, a lesson that Abraham knew all too well. But as he demonstrated, walking in obedience to God's calling can lead to profound blessings and purpose. Abraham, revered as the father of many nations, epitomizes obedience. He left his homeland when God called, believed in God's promise of a son in his old age, and was even willing to sacrifice this son. In recognition of his profound faith, God spared Isaac.

Your True Self

In today's world, you often grapple with many choices, making it challenging to discern which paths align with God's will. Peer pressure, societal expectations, and personal desires can often cloud judgment. But much like Abraham, who faced the ultimate test of obedience, your own choices often test your resolve and faith. But by seeking God's guidance and choosing obedience, clarity and direction emerge.

Sierra's Song

Sierra's voice had the rare ability to transport listeners to another world. It wasn't just the pitch-perfect notes or the impressive range; it was the soul she poured into every word. Her gift was a blessing, and much like Abraham, she felt a divine calling to use it rightly. From an early age, she felt her gift was divinely bestowed, and she often dreamt of singing in the church choir, touching souls, and lifting spirits.

As she honed her talent through the years, opportunities started knocking. Among her opportunities was an offer from Celestial Beats, a popular band. Facing such a crossroads was Sierra's "Isaac moment," a challenge to her obedience to her initial divine calling. The offer? To be their lead vocalist, promising tours, fame, a lavish lifestyle, and fans by the thousands.

It was everything a budding artist could wish for. Sierra found herself on the verge of the glittering world of music, with all its allure laid out before her. And yet, a quiet voice within her whispered of her childhood dreams—of the church's echoing hall, the serene melodies, and the peace it brought to her heart.

Torn between the two worlds, Sierra turned to prayer. Nights were spent in reflection, seeking guidance. Like Abraham, she sought God's will in her life, wanting her decisions to be in line with His desires. The band's offer was time-bound, and the clock was ticking. Her friends, excited about the potential fame, couldn't fathom her hesitation. But Sierra sought a deeper, more meaningful connection through her music.

One evening, as she sat in the church, the choir began practicing a hymn. The profound lyrics, the harmonious voices resonating in the sacred space, brought tears to her eyes. It was a moment of clarity. It was her Moriah, her moment of true obedience to God's call. She realized she yearned for the fulfillment that came from touching hearts, not just pleasing ears.

Mustering her courage, Sierra declined the band's offer. Instead, she joined the church choir, pouring her soul into hymns and gospel songs, elevating the spiritual experience of the congregation. In her obedience, much like Abraham, Sierra found a deeper connection with God and her true purpose. There were no roaring crowds or flashing camera lights, but the glow in the eyes of the elderly, the comfort her voice provided to the troubled, and the upliftment she felt within herself surpassed any fame she could have achieved.

God, it seemed, had His plans for Sierra. A couple of years into her service, a producer attended a Sunday service, captivated by Sierra's ethereal voice. He approached her with a unique proposition: a series of spiritual albums, aimed at providing solace and hope.

Sierra's albums became an unexpected sensation. They weren't just chart-toppers, but were played in hospitals, shelters, and homes, providing comfort to souls worldwide. By walking in obedience, Sierra reaped blessings that mirrored the profound promises God made to Abraham after his ultimate act of faith. Her songs of faith and devotion touched lives in ways she hadn't imagined.

In an interview, when asked about her earlier choice, Sierra said, "The fame I might have gained with the band could never match the fulfillment I've found in this path. I chose to serve God, and in doing so, I found my true purpose."

Sierra's journey underscores the power of heeding one's divine calling. Despite the world's noise, Sierra listened to her inner voice and, in doing so, found her most authentic self.

Daily Dose of Faith

* **Guided Meditation:** Start your day with a five-minute meditation, focusing on listening and opening your heart to God's will.

* **Scripture Study:** Dedicate time each week to delve deeper into biblical stories of obedience, drawing lessons and inspiration.

* **Seek Counsel:** Talk to mentors, church leaders, or trusted adults about decisions you face, seeking their godly advice.

Living the Faith

Like Abraham, Sierra's faith-guided choice touched many souls. Her voice became an instrument of worship, bringing solace and inspiration to others. While she didn't tour the world, she impacted her community profoundly, finding joy in her purpose.

Journal Time!

* Reflect on a time when you faced a tough choice. Did you seek God's guidance? What was the outcome?

* What does obedience mean to you? Is it a burden or a blessing?

* Write a prayer asking God to grant you the wisdom and courage to walk in obedience, even when the path seems challenging.

* Are there areas where you struggle to be obedient? What holds you back?

Wrapping Up the Week

While obedience might be viewed as traditional, its core values and rewards are timeless. In the grand scheme of life, walking in obedience to God's will, like Abraham did, brings not only blessings but also a deeper sense of purpose. The world might offer fleeting moments of pleasure, but God offers eternal joy and fulfillment.

Week 40: Live Out Your Faith Boldly

"For I am not ashamed of the gospel, because it is the power of God that brings salvation to everyone who believes."

—Romans 1:16

Recommended Reading:
The story of Jael (Judges 4:17–22)

Boldness in faith is about having the courage to stand firm in your beliefs, even when faced with opposition. It's about having the courage to stand firm in your beliefs, even in the face of opposition, and to openly live according to those convictions. It means speaking out, living authentically according to your beliefs, just as Jael did when she made a game-changing decision.

Jael, not an Israelite by birth, made a choice to stand with the Israelites against their oppressors, showcasing her alignment with the God of Israel. Her decision to drive a tent peg into the enemy commander's temple was a defining moment that led to victory for the Israelites. While her violent action may be morally complex, it underscored her deep commitment and boldness in aligning with what she saw as righteousness.

Your True Self

In today's digital age, with the influx of diverse opinions and the fear of backlash, it's tempting to follow the majority and suppress your unique voice, particularly on topics as personal as faith. Just as Jael had to make a critical choice that defied expectations, you will face your own challenges. The pressure to fit in can be overpowering. Yet, deep down, amid the chaos of life, there's a genuine self, a core identity, that seeks grounding in profound beliefs and values.

Lakshmi's Leap of Faith

Lakshmi's life had always been rooted in faith. Growing up, she felt the comforting embrace of her beliefs, guiding her through challenges and lighting up her path. Yet, there were moments when she felt the weight of external judgment, not unlike Jael, who might have faced skepticism or criticism for her actions. But, fearing potential judgment or misunderstanding, sharing this crucial part of herself with her close-knit group of friends became a challenge she hadn't yet faced. While her friends spoke freely of weekend plans, hobbies, and personal dramas, Lakshmi's stories of spiritual reflections remained locked within.

Taking inspiration from Jael, Lakshmi understood the importance of action and alignment with faith, even in moments of uncertainty or fear. It wasn't that she was ashamed. Far from it. It was the gnawing fear of being perceived differently, of being labeled or misunderstood, that muzzled her. Conversations on religion and faith often became polarized, and Lakshmi dreaded the thought of drifting away from friends due to a difference in beliefs.

One sunny afternoon, as she walked through the park, she spotted Jamie, one of her closest friends, seated alone on a bench, her face buried in her hands. Drawing closer, Lakshmi realized Jamie was crying. Offering a comforting arm, she waited for Jamie to share what had caused her such distress.

Jamie began talking about how lost she felt lately, how every choice seemed like a misstep and the future appeared so dauntingly uncertain. As Lakshmi listened, every fiber of her being wanted to share the solace she found in her faith, the stories of guidance and strength. But the familiar chains of hesitation held her back.

It was then that she remembered a sermon she had once heard, emphasizing the importance of being a model for others, of shining one's light. Taking a deep breath, Lakshmi decided to break free from her self-imposed silence.

She began by acknowledging Jamie's feelings, then gently started recounting her personal journey—the times when she had felt directionless, the moments when her faith had served as her compass. Lakshmi spoke of the comfort she drew from her beliefs, the hope it instilled in her even in the darkest hours. It was a heartfelt sharing of her own experiences, a bridge of understanding she hoped to build with Jamie. It was a candid heart-to-heart, sharing the sources of her strength.

To Lakshmi's surprise, Jamie didn't pull away or look uncomfortable. Instead, her eyes reflected a genuine curiosity. This moment mirrored the reactions of many who heard Paul's teachings; an unexpected openness to understanding and connection. As Lakshmi concluded her story, Jamie's eyes glistened, absorbing every word, and a heavy silence wrapped around them. Then, Jamie whispered, "Thank you, Lakshmi. I needed to hear that. Not necessarily the faith aspect, but the assurance that there's hope, that there are anchors in life we can hold onto."

From that day, Lakshmi understood that, just as messages of hope and faith have resonated throughout history, her own genuine sharing of her journey could touch others deeply. It was about sharing, relating, and sometimes, just offering another perspective. Her courage to open up about her faith didn't push her friends away. Instead, it added another layer to their understanding of her. Most importantly, it reinforced

Lakshmi's belief that being genuine and bold in expressing one's identity, including one's faith, can touch lives in unexpected ways.

Daily Dose of Faith

* **Affirmation Cards:** Write down Bible verses or affirmations that inspire you to be bold. Carry one with you every day.

* **Faith Partner:** Find a friend who shares your faith. Together, challenge each other to acts of boldness each week.

* **Sharing Your Story:** Talk about your faith journey with someone close, or write down your personal testimony to reflect upon.

Living the Faith

Just as Jael's bold decision had profound repercussions, Lakshmi's own story became a catalyst for others to explore and understand faith. Similarly, by sharing her story, Lakshmi inspired many in her school to consider the impact of faith. Some joined youth groups, while others approached her with questions. Through her actions, she created ripples that affected those around her.

Journal Time!

* Think about a time when you felt the urge to speak about your faith, but hesitated. What held you back?

* What does "boldness" mean to you? Is it speaking out, acting differently, or something else?

* Imagine a scenario where your faith was challenged. How would you respond boldly, but lovingly?

* List people in your life who exemplify boldness in faith. What can you learn from them?

Wrapping Up the Week

Like Jael, you too have the power to influence others through the bold expression of your faith. Remember, your voice, your story, can be a source of inspiration and guidance for many. This week, challenge yourself to find one way to live out your faith boldly and share it with someone close.

Week 41: Find Joy in the Journey

*"You make known to me the path of life;
you will fill me with joy in your presence,
with eternal pleasures at your right hand."*
—Psalm 16:11

Recommended Reading:
The story of Paul and Silas singing in jail (Acts 16:16–40)

Trials and tribulations are a part of life. But how you choose to react to these challenges defines your journey. Like the Psalmist, Paul and Silas found joy in the presence of God. While in the city of Philippi, Paul and Silas were imprisoned after they cast a spirit out of a girl, angering those who profited from her fortune-telling abilities. Instead of lamenting their situation, they chose to sing hymns to God. Around midnight, as their songs of praise echoed, a massive earthquake shook the prison, releasing all the prisoners from their chains. Their unwavering faith and joy, even in adversity, not only inspired their fellow inmates but also led to the jailer and his family turning to Christ.

Your True Self

Societal pressures might often make you feel that showing vulnerability or sadness is a sign of weakness. This is amplified with the fear of being left out or misunderstood. But true strength comes from embracing every emotion, understanding it, and finding joy even in the hardest moments. It's the kind of joy Paul and Silas found, even behind prison walls.

Lethabo's Digital Hymnal

Lethabo's life buzzed with constant activity. From volleyball practices after school to weekend hangouts with her tight-knit group of friends, she thrived on connection and camaraderie. Her laughter could light up any room, and her spirit never wavered. Yet, when the statewide lockdown came into effect, the ceaseless motion screeched to an unsettling halt.

In the confines of her room, Lethabo faced a challenge akin to Paul and Silas's prison cell—isolation. Her sunlit room, adorned with trophies, posters, and cherished memories, now felt more like a cage. The joy she once found in her home was overshadowed by the echoing silence of the empty streets outside. She missed the casual hugs, the unplanned meetups, and the euphoria of scoring a point in a closely fought match.

The first few days were the hardest. The unfamiliar void threatened to swallow her spirit, and the weight of isolation pressed down on her chest, making it hard to breathe. News feeds were filled with grim updates, casting a constant shadow over Lethabo's mind. Anxiety wrapped around her like a suffocating shroud.

One Sunday morning, as she aimlessly scrolled through her phone, Lethabo stumbled upon a video from her Sunday school, a story about using one's talents to uplift spirits. The protagonist had played his violin on a balcony during a challenging time in his community, soothing stressed souls with his melodies. The story struck a chord in her. She was reminded of how Paul and Silas used their gift of song to find joy and inspire others, even in captivity.

Lethabo had always loved singing, her voice serving as a comforting escape during difficult times. Remembering the story, she had an idea. With the world outside her window silent, she decided to fill her digital world with music. Setting up her phone camera, she took a deep breath and began singing a hymn she had always found solace in.

She was hesitant at first, unsure about sharing such a personal moment. But the uplifting lyrics and her genuine emotion seemed to resonate, creating an atmosphere of hope in her room. When she finished, she uploaded the video online, hoping it might comfort someone as it did her.

The response was overwhelming. Messages poured in from acquaintances, friends, and even strangers, all expressing how her song had brought light to their gloomy days. It was as if she had echoed the same joy that Paul and Silas shared in their prison cell. A neighbor mentioned hearing her voice and joining in from his balcony. A friend's mom shared how the hymn reminded her of better days. With every message, Lethabo's heart swelled with warmth.

Inspired, Lethabo made it a ritual. Every week, she would pick a new hymn, practice it, and then share it online. The process not only gave her a purpose but also recreated a sense of community in the virtual world. What started as a simple attempt to combat her own loneliness transformed into a beacon of hope for many.

When the lockdown lifted and life began returning to normal, Lethabo's digital hymnal had already created ripples. Her bonds with her friends were stronger, and her community more tightly knit than before.

In the midst of a world forced into silence, Lethabo had found her voice, turning a challenging chapter in her life into an anthem of hope and resilience. She embodied Psalm 16:11, finding joy in her journey, much like Paul and Silas had.

Daily Dose of Faith

* **Playlist of Joy:** Create a playlist of songs that uplift your spirit. Turn to it whenever you need a boost.

* **Gratitude Journal:** Each day, write down three things you're grateful for. Over time, you'll start focusing on the positives more.

* **Reach Out:** Share your feelings with someone you trust. Sometimes, just vocalizing your emotions brings clarity and joy.

Living the Faith

Inspired by her newfound love for singing hymns, Lethabo started a virtual choir group. They would meet online once a week, choosing hymns that spoke of hope and joy. These hymns were a testament to the fact that joy can be found on any journey, just as Paul and Silas found it in theirs. This group brought light to many, turning the isolation into a period of spiritual growth.

Journal Time!

* Think of a situation where you felt trapped or helpless. How did you cope? Could you find any joy during that time?

* How can singing or listening to uplifting music change your mood or perspective?

* Describe a moment when you witnessed someone finding joy in an unlikely situation. How did it impact you?

* If you were to write a song or poem about finding joy among challenges, what would the first line be?

Wrapping Up the Week

As you move through your days, remember that joy is often a choice you make. Take inspiration from Paul, Silas, and Lethabo: seek joy, cherish it, and let it radiate to those around you. Your journey is your song; make sure it sings of hope and joy.

Week 42: Embrace Rest

"Remember the Sabbath day by keeping it holy.
Six days you shall labor and do all your work, but the
seventh day is a Sabbath to the Lord your God.
On it you shall not do any work."
—Exodus 20:8–10

Recommended Readings:
To explore the concept of rest, rejuvenation, and the importance of sacred pauses, consider the following passages: Exodus 20:8–11 and Matthew 14:22–23.

In Matthew 11:28–29, Jesus says, "Come to me, all you who are weary and burdened, and I will give you rest. Take my yoke upon you and learn from me, for I am gentle and humble in heart, and you will find rest for your souls."

Throughout His busy ministry, Jesus still found moments of solitude. He often withdrew to quiet places to pray and rest. This behavior mirrors the essence of the Sabbath, as highlighted in Exodus. One notable instance is after feeding five thousand people. Instead of basking in the success of the event, Jesus went up on a mountainside alone to pray and find solitude. His actions serve as a powerful reminder of the need for personal time and rest in your life.

Your True Self

You live in a world that glorifies "busy." In today's hyper-connected world, there's a mounting pressure to always be "on." The pull of social media, school, and societal expectations can be overwhelming. It's crucial to remember the importance of rest—not just for your physical well-being, but for your spiritual and emotional health too. Drawing wisdom from Exodus, there's a divine directive about the importance of rest. But there's a sacredness in slowing down, in taking a moment to just be. Jesus, in all his divinity and with the weight of His mission, still took the time to rest and rejuvenate. You too can find strength in these sacred pauses.

Amber's Sabbath

Amber's life was a precisely tuned symphony of obligations. Just as the Israelites were commanded to remember the Sabbath, Amber too had lost sight of this divine rhythm of rest. Between debates, advanced physics, and shifts at the town's bookstore, every minute of her day was meticulously plotted. Friends admired her, teachers praised her, and parents beamed with pride. To everyone, she was the epitome of a successful high school senior.

But the portrait was beginning to crack.

It started subtly: a forgotten assignment here, a postponed hangout there. Amber's buoyant spirit that once led her school's pep rallies began to dwindle. Mornings grew heavier, nights more restless. The reflection in the mirror seemed more haggard, the eyes more distant. As the weeks rolled on, the lustrous aura of her achievements began to pale in comparison to the mounting exhaustion.

It was during a youth group meeting, one she almost skipped out of sheer fatigue, that things began to shift. Sister Rose-Marie, the group's leader, narrated a tale not of Jesus's miracles or sermons, but of his rest. She painted a picture that paralleled Jesus's actions with the Sabbath, emphasizing the importance of rest as Jesus himself demonstrated. "Even Jesus," she began, "in the whirlwind of His ministry, understood the need to retreat, to rejuvenate, and to find solace away from the ceaseless demands of the world."

Amber listened intently as Sister Rose-Marie described how Jesus would often escape to quiet places, seeking communion with nature and God. "He understood," she continued, "that to serve others, one must first ensure they are filled with God's peace and strength."

That night, Amber lay in bed pondering. Here she was, burning the candle at both ends, while even the Son of God understood the significance of taking a break. Echoing Matthew 11:28–29, Amber felt Jesus's call to embrace rest. The realization was simple, yet profound.

She needed a change.

The very next week, Amber marked her calendar: Saturday, from sunrise to sunset, would be her day of rest. She was choosing to honor the concept of the Sabbath, a day dedicated to rejuvenation and connection with God. No studying, no shifts, no obligations. Just Amber, her thoughts, and whatever she felt like doing—or not doing.

The first Saturday was oddly challenging. She caught herself reaching for her textbooks, her fingers itching to check emails. But with every passing hour, she began to reacquaint herself with the world outside her obligations. She read a novel for the sheer pleasure of it, took a languid walk through the local park, and even attempted baking, resulting in somewhat lopsided muffins.

By evening, as she sat on her porch sipping tea, she felt a tranquility she hadn't experienced in years. Her thoughts were clearer, her body more relaxed, and her spirit, once burdened, now felt lighter.

As weeks turned to months, Amber's day of rest became her anchor. Her grades rebounded, her friendships deepened, and her zest for life returned. In embracing the biblical teaching of rest, Amber discovered a spiritual and emotional oasis. Friends and family noticed the change, remarking on her renewed vigor and joy. And while her schedule remained full, her soul no longer felt depleted.

When graduation came, Amber was, unsurprisingly, the valedictorian. In her speech, she didn't just celebrate achievements and future aspirations. Instead, she spoke of balance, drawing inspiration from the teachings of Exodus and the examples set by Jesus.

Amber's journey taught her that true success isn't measured by continuous activity, but by recognizing when to pause. It was about understanding that, in the vast expanse of life's obligations, true fulfillment often lies in the moments you choose to pause.

Daily Dose of Faith

* **Tech Detox:** Much like Amber's "Restful Saturdays," dedicate a day to be free from digital distractions."

* **Nature Walk:** Follow Amber's example by taking a tranquil walk to reconnect with nature and God.

* **Meditative Moments:** Find your mountainside, much like Jesus did, to pray and reflect.

Living the Faith

Wanting to share the solace she found in her personal rest days, Amber began organizing "Restful Saturdays" with her friends. This was her way of sharing the biblical principle of Sabbath with others. They'd picnic in the park, read books, share stories, and relish in the simple pleasures—recharging not just their bodies, but their souls too.

Journal Time!

* How do you currently prioritize rest in your daily routine?

* What activities genuinely relax and rejuvenate you?

* How does taking a break help you connect more deeply with God and yourself?

* Reflect on a time when you felt burnt out. What changes can you make to ensure you embrace rest in the future?

Wrapping Up the Week

Rest isn't merely an absence of activity; it's an intentional rejuvenation of your spirit. By embracing moments of stillness and calm, you align yourself more closely with God's design for your life. As you remember the Sabbath and heed Jesus's call for rest, you find rejuvenation and deeper connection with the Divine. Just as Jesus took moments for solitude and reflection, so should you, to nourish your soul and continue your journey with renewed vigor.

Week 43: Pray for Others

"Therefore confess your sins to each other and pray for each other so that you may be healed. The prayer of a righteous person is powerful and effective."

—James 5:16

> **Recommended Reading:**
> The story of Nehemiah (Nehemiah 1:4–11)

When facing challenges, whether personal or concerning those you care about, the Bible emphasizes the transformative power of prayer. Just as Nehemiah felt a deep sense of responsibility and turned to fervent prayer for his people, you too can be conduits of God's healing through your intercession.

Often, when your loved ones face troubles, you can feel powerless. But there's a strength you can tap into, a way to support—through prayer. Nehemiah, despite his distance, prayed passionately for his people, and his story illuminates the power of intercession.

Nehemiah, a Jew serving as a cupbearer to the king in a foreign land, was deeply connected to his homeland and its people. Despite being in a distant land, when he heard of the struggles and despair his people faced in Jerusalem, his heart was heavy. Rather than feeling helpless, he turned to prayer. For days, he mourned, fasted, and prayed for his city and its people. Nehemiah's prayers were heartfelt, and he asked God not only for help but also for forgiveness.

He then took inspired action, approaching the king with his concerns and embarking on a mission to rebuild Jerusalem's walls. Nehemiah's story is a testament to how prayer and action can change the course of history.

Your True Self

Drawing parallels from Nehemiah's dedication to his people, in today's world where solutions are often sought externally, prayer reminds you of the internal power you possess. Intercessory prayer isn't just about asking God for favors; it's a deep expression of love and concern for others. In the same vein as Nehemiah, who channeled his distress into intercession, you can also direct your worries and concerns for your loved ones into meaningful prayers.

The Power of Prayer

Kamilah sat in her room, phone in hand, trying to digest the words she'd just heard. Chloe, her childhood best friend, was going through a stormy phase at home. Their bond, built over shared secrets and countless sleepovers, meant Chloe's pain resonated deeply within Kamilah. She felt an overwhelming mix of emotions: sympathy, anger, but most of all, helplessness. For all their shared history, this was a battle she couldn't directly intervene in.

Every day, as Kamilah went about her routines, she felt Chloe's shadows looming. They shared lunch at school, their chats filled with inconsequential subjects, but Kamilah could sense the weight behind Chloe's eyes, the strain in her voice. Numerous times, Kamilah offered a comforting hand, a listening ear, even a place to stay. But the depth of Chloe's family issues couldn't be washed away with sleepovers and ice cream.

Kamilah's heart ached, much like Nehemiah's did for Jerusalem, feeling the urge to do something significant. One chilly evening, Kamilah found herself at her bedroom window, gazing at the vast expanse of stars. She remembered her grandmother's words about the power of prayer, how it could be a bridge when physical intervention seemed impossible. Tentatively, she whispered a prayer for Chloe.

This soon became a sacred ritual. Every evening, just after sunset, Kamilah would sit in a quiet corner, close her eyes, and speak her heart out. Every evening, Kamilah would sit in a quiet corner, immersing herself in earnest prayers for Chloe; she poured her heart out to God on behalf of her friend. She prayed for strength, resilience, and love for Chloe. She asked for healing in her friend's household, for understanding, and most of all, for peace.

As days turned into weeks, something remarkable began to unfold. Chloe's demeanor started to shift. The weight in her eyes began to lift, and there was a newfound spring in her step. She began sharing snippets of improvement at home, of conversations that led to understanding, and of hope rekindling.

Kamilah was elated. While she hadn't expected overnight miracles, she felt a connection between her earnest prayers and Chloe's improving circumstances. But more than that, through this process, Kamilah discovered something profound within herself. These dedicated moments of prayer, which began as a means to assist Chloe, had become an introspective journey for Kamilah. This journey of intercessory prayer allowed Kamilah to explore the depth of her commitment, faith, and love for her friend. She felt more connected to her faith, to Chloe, and to the world around her.

One evening, as the two girls sat on Kamilah's porch, wrapped in cozy blankets and sipping hot chocolate, Chloe said, "Becca, I don't know how to explain it, but lately, I've felt this incredible energy surrounding me. It's like an invisible force is holding me, guiding me."

Kamilah smiled gently, squeezing Chloe's hand. "Sometimes," she whispered, "we find strength in the most unexpected places."

As the months rolled on, Chloe's home life became more stable. The two girls, now even closer, often reminisced about that challenging period, cherishing the bond it had fortified. Their bond had weathered storms, and it was evident that faith and love, even when unseen, had the power to heal and restore. And while Chloe might never know the full extent of Kamilah's nightly prayers, their friendship stood as a testament to the unseen forces of faith, love, and the enduring power of connection.

Daily Dose of Faith

* **Dedicated Time:** Set aside a specific time each day to pray for others.
* **Prayer List:** Keep a list of those in need of prayers. It helps to focus your intentions.
* **Group Prayer:** Join or form a group where you collectively pray for others. There's strength in numbers.

Living in Faith

Drawing inspiration from her own experiences and the stories of faith she had learned, Kamilah started a "Prayer Partners" group at her school, where teens came together once a week to pray for each other and their community. The group became a haven of support, love, and understanding.

Journal Time!

* Who in your life needs prayer support right now?
* How does it feel when you set aside time to pray for others?
* Can you recall a time when someone may have prayed for you, and it made a difference?
* How can you integrate intercessory prayer into your daily routine?

Wrapping Up the Week

Praying for others extends a bridge of compassion, love, and hope. It's an act that not only benefits those you pray for but also strengthens your bond with God. Nehemiah's steadfast commitment to prayer and his consequent actions teach you that even in times of distress, your prayers combined with action can lead to monumental changes.

Week 44: Build Unity in Diversity

"There is neither Jew nor Gentile, neither slave nor free, nor is there male and female, for you are all one in Christ Jesus."
—Galatians 3:28

> **Recommended Reading:**
> The story of the Tower of Babel (Genesis 11)

In a world filled with a myriad of cultures, languages, and traditions, understanding and unity can sometimes seem out of reach. While the Tower of Babel story depicts division, it also offers lessons on unity in diversity. Much like how the people in the story were divided due to their pride, it's our collective humility and understanding that can unite us once again.

In Genesis 11, with one language, humanity aimed to build a tower for their glory, not God's. Their pride led God to diversify their language, scattering them worldwide. This story, though seen as a division, is also the birth of our diverse cultures and languages. It reminds you that in our pursuits, our purpose should align with God's will and that diversity is a gift, not a curse.

Your True Self

Teens like you are exposed to global influences more than any previous generation. With the internet, travel, and multicultural societies, there's beauty in diversity. However, understanding and respect are paramount. It's crucial to remember that in the face of our differences, you must seek unity, just as the Bible teaches you. You shouldn't aim to be the same, but to appreciate various cultures and backgrounds.

The Mosaic of Unity

Dalal's eyes sparkled with excitement as she walked through the school's corridors, admiring the posters announcing the annual cultural festival. With a student body representing over twenty different nationalities, the festival was a vibrant patchwork of traditions, dances, food, and music. This year, Dalal was determined to showcase the vibrant history and rich traditions of her Palestinian heritage. She wanted to highlight unity, much like the biblical principle of all being one in Christ.

But as preparations got underway, the atmosphere grew tense. The large hall echoed with heated debates and clashing opinions. It was almost as if the confusion of Babel had revisited them. The Indian group was arguing about the best dance form to showcase; the Nigerian students were trying to negotiate between different tribal displays. Language barriers added to the confusion. The Japanese students felt left out, the French group was struggling with their menu, and the Chilean students were torn between two folk songs. The cacophony was overwhelming, and the festival seemed on the brink of collapse.

Dalal watched, heart sinking, as the elaborate fabric threatened to fray. She thought back to the Tower of Babel, where a united humanity ended in confusion. But she also believed in a hopeful future of unity in diversity, as highlighted by Galatians 3:28. She realized that instead of a celebration of diversity, the festival was becoming a battleground of egos and misunderstandings.

One evening, as Dalal was helping her grandmother clean the attic, she stumbled upon a beautiful old mosaic. The ceramic tiles, seemingly disparate at first glance, came together to form a radiant pattern. An idea began to take shape in her mind.

The next day, she approached the student committee with a proposal: Why not create a giant mosaic mural for the festival? Each group could contribute a piece that represented their culture, and together, they would assemble these pieces into one cohesive artwork. In her heart, Dalal was inspired by the unity preached in Galatians and the lessons of unity in diversity from Babel. The mural would be a testament to the school's diverse student body, symbolizing unity within diversity.

At first, the idea was met with skepticism. Dalal's passion ignited a spark in others. The Mexican group offered brightly colored Talavera tiles; the Egyptian students contributed pieces with hieroglyphic patterns. The Chinese group painted delicate porcelain shards, while the Russians added tiles with folkloric designs. As each group started working on their contributions, the atmosphere shifted from one of competition to one of collaboration.

Under Dalal's guidance, they began assembling the mural in the school's central courtyard. Bit by bit, the pieces began to fit together. The vibrant hues, the myriad patterns, and the diverse textures created artwork that was more magnificent than anything they could've achieved individually.

As the festival dawned, the curtain fell away from the mural, drawing collective gasps and eyes widening in admiration. Parents, teachers, and students stood in awe, tracing the patterns, marveling at the seamless fusion of cultures. Each tile told a story, yet they all came together to form a single narrative of unity.

The festival continued with performances, food stalls, and exhibitions, but the mosaic mural was the undeniable star. It was a testament to the power of collaboration, of looking beyond differences, and finding common ground.

The legacy of that festival endured. Even years after Dalal graduated, the mural remained, reminding everyone of the unity achieved that day. And while many stories were told about that day, the most enduring was of a Palestinian girl with a vision—a vision that transformed discord into harmony, bridging gaps with tiles and mortar, and teaching a community the true essence of unity in diversity.

Daily Dose of Faith

Remember the Tower of Babel and strive to bring unity in your community.

* **Educate Yourself:** Take time to learn about a new culture every month.

* **Communication:** When misunderstandings arise, approach them with a heart to understand, not to argue.

* **Celebrate Differences:** Attend multicultural festivals, eat diverse cuisines, and participate in cultural exchanges.

Living the Faith

Following the success of the mural, Dalal's school started a "Culture Club" where every month, students from a specific cultural background would share their traditions, food, and stories. Drawing inspiration from the early Christian message of unity, this became a bridge, fostering understanding and friendships among diverse groups.

Journal Time!

* Reflect on a time when cultural differences enriched your life.

* How do you feel when confronted with a culture you're unfamiliar with?

* Share a time when you felt out of place because of cultural differences. How did you handle it?

* How can you bridge cultural divides in your community? Describe a moment when unity overcame division in your life.

Wrapping Up the Week

Diversity is God's masterpiece—a spectrum of colors and cultures painting our world. Through stories like Babel and Galatians 3:28's message, you're reminded of our collective unity in the face of our beautiful differences. We are all one, no matter our backgrounds. Embrace each unique piece, knowing that together, we create a beautiful mosaic of humanity.

Week 45: Learn to Listen

*"My dear brothers and sisters, take note of this:
Everyone should be quick to listen, slow to speak
and slow to become angry."*
—James 1:19

Recommended Reading:
The story of Rebekah (Genesis 24)

In your fast-paced world filled with constant notifications, multimedia overload, and competing demands on your time, the deep and genuine art of listening often gets overshadowed. But as the story of Rebekah demonstrates, sometimes the most significant guidance comes not from grand gestures but from careful listening and following divine signs.

In Genesis 24, Rebekah listens intently to Abraham's servant recount how God had directed him to find a wife for Isaac. Moved by his words and the unfolding of God's plan, Rebekah agrees to return with him and marry Isaac. Her attentiveness and openness to God's plan underscore the importance of listening and being receptive to divine signs.

Your True Self

The pressures of today's world might condition you to be reactive. You might be used to instant messaging, quick solutions, and rapid responses. Much like Rebekah, you might need to discern the divine signs or the genuine needs of others, looking beyond the immediate to grasp deeper truths. But in the rush, you might miss the subtleties, the unsaid emotions, and God's gentle nudges. True connection, with both God and others, requires you to cultivate the skill of attentive listening.

The Art of Listening

Maddie was the problem solver, the go-to person in her circle for advice. It wasn't just a role she'd been given; it was one she embraced. Whenever troubles brewed, Maddie's voice was the steady anchor, preventing friends from drifting into turbulent waters. She was always ready to intervene with her own "wind, earthquake, or fire." Especially when it came to Jade, her best friend since childhood.

One particularly crisp autumn afternoon, as golden leaves danced around their favorite park bench, Jade began to open up about the growing tension at home. Maddie, ever the savior, immediately began suggesting ways to mediate the disputes, offering tips to create peace, and even proposing self-help books that might be helpful. She was so intent on being the strong gust of wind or the shaking earthquake with her advice. She spoke with fervor, sure that her advice was the raft Jade needed in these troubled waters.

Jade, however, remained quiet, occasionally nodding. As Maddie talked, she stared at the leaves, her face a blend of sadness and frustration.

When Maddie finally ran out of solutions, Jade turned to her, tears glistening in her eyes. "Mads," she began softly, "Sometimes, I don't need solutions. Sometimes, I just need an ear. I need you to listen, truly listen, without immediately trying to fix things."

Maddie blinked, taken aback. She realized she had been dominating the narrative, when all Jade needed was the silent solidarity of a close friend. Taking a deep breath, Maddie gently squeezed Jade's hand. "I'm sorry," she whispered, her voice choked with emotion. "I promise, from now on, I'll listen more and speak less."

216

Jade smiled weakly, squeezing back. "It's okay. I know you mean well. But sometimes, the weight lifts a bit just by sharing, you know? Not everything needs a solution."

The two sat in silence for a while, watching the leaves, feeling the heaviness of the moment. It was a pivotal point in their friendship, a lesson learned in the most unexpected of ways.

Weeks turned into months, and the dynamics between the two friends shifted subtly. Maddie practiced the art of listening more. She learned to discern when Jade needed advice and when she just needed an understanding ear. Their conversations deepened, becoming more raw, more authentic.

One evening, as they sat on the same park bench, Jade said, "You know, Mads, our chats lately have been a balm for me. Thank you for just... being there."

Maddie smiled, squeezing her friend's hand. "Always," she whispered.

In that quiet park, with the leaves rustling, much like Rebekah in her moment of decision, two friends discovered the profound strength in silence, in merely being present. Maddie realized that sometimes, the most potent words were the ones left unsaid, and that often, the best way to be there for someone was just to listen.

Daily Dose of Faith

* **Mindful Listening:** Practice being fully present by maintaining eye contact, turning off or silencing devices, and focusing solely on the speaker's words and emotions.

* **Silent Moments with God:** Dedicate a few minutes daily to sit in silence, much like Rebekah did when discerning God's plan, inviting God to speak to your heart.

* **Refrain from Interrupting:** Let others express themselves fully before you respond.

Living the Faith

Maddie took Jade's words to heart. She started practicing listening—not just to her friends but in her prayer life too. Instead of inundating her prayers with requests, she began to sit silently, seeking the still, small voice of God. This transformed her relationships and deepened her connection with God.

Journal Time!

* Reflect on a time you felt truly listened to. What did the other person do specifically that made you feel understood and valued?

* Do you find it challenging to sit in silence? Why?

* Describe a situation where you wish you had listened more carefully.

* How can you cultivate a better listening relationship with God and those around you?

Wrapping Up the Week

In a world that often screams for your attention, choosing to listen—truly listen—can be a revolutionary act. Whether it's tuning into a friend's unspoken pain, discerning the signs and directions like Rebekah did, or hearing God's gentle guidance, mastering the art of listening enriches your relationships and deepens your faith. As you journey through this week, strive to be someone who not only hears but truly understands and connects with the hearts of others. Challenge yourself to embrace the quiet moments, to be present, and to value the power of a listening ear.

Week 46: Overcome Discouragement

"Why, my soul, are you downcast? Why so disturbed within me? Put your hope in God, for I will yet praise him, my Savior and my God."

—Psalm 42:11

Recommended Reading:
The story of Abigail (1 Samuel 25)

Discouragement can creep in like shadows lengthening at dusk, making your challenges feel insurmountable. But as Abigail's story illustrates, with wisdom and diplomacy, you can navigate even the most challenging situations with grace.

In the first book of Samuel, Abigail shows sensibility and courage. Despite living with a difficult husband, she acted with intelligence and foresight, intervening to prevent a deadly conflict between her husband, Nabal, and David. Her story is a testament to the power of wisdom and peace-making in overcoming discouragement.

Your True Self

In today's competitive world, you might be under constant pressure to excel academically, socially, and in extracurriculars. A small setback can seem like the end of the world. Similar to Abigail, who faced tension with diplomacy, you, too, might face situations that require tact and grace. However, setbacks are just setups for comebacks. You can find the resilience to rise above discouragement by relying on your faith.

Doubt and Triumph on the Volleyball Court

The echoing thud of the volleyball smacking the court was a constant reminder to Cassidy of her team's missteps. As captain, every point lost, every misjudged pass, and every failed serve weighed heavily on her shoulders. The annual interschool championship was approaching, and the weight of expectations loomed large. To make matters worse, her team had lost three practice matches in a row.

With her infectious enthusiasm and undeniable skill, Cassidy had once been a source of inspiration for her teammates. But just like Abigail, who navigated a tense situation with David, Cassidy now felt the weight of responsibility, constantly second-guessing her decisions on the court. While she diligently watched match replays late into the night, seeking areas of improvement, she found herself swayed by doubt.

After another discouraging practice, Cassidy sat slumped on the bleachers, questioning her ability to lead. Noticing her despondency, Coach Martinez approached her.

"I've been coaching for two decades," began Coach Martinez, "and I've seen many players like you, Cassidy. Talented, dedicated, but weighed down by their own expectations."

Cassidy looked over, tears brimming in her eyes. "I don't know if I can do it, Coach. Maybe I'm not cut out for this."

Coach Martinez smiled gently, "You remind me of Abigail."

Cassidy frowned in confusion. "Who?"

"A biblical figure. Abigail was a woman of wisdom who intervened to prevent a deadly conflict. She understood the bigger picture and acted with grace and diplomacy."

Cassidy listened, intrigued.

Coach continued, "It wasn't just her wisdom but her courage that stood out. She approached a potentially volatile situation with calmness and tact."

Cassidy pondered Coach Martinez's words, the story of Abigail resonating deeply within her.

"You have that same grace and wisdom, Cassidy," Coach said. "Your team believes in you. Now, it's time you believe in yourself."

Drawing strength from Abigail's diplomacy and tact, Cassidy began approaching training with a renewed sense of purpose. The day of the interschool championship arrived, and Cassidy's team played with a cohesion and spirit that left spectators in awe. Lifting the championship trophy, Cassidy knew that her journey of self-belief, inspired by a biblical tale, was the true victory.

Daily Dose of Faith

*   **Reflect & Reframe:** Instead of focusing on what went wrong, think of what you learned.

*   **Seek Support:** Talk to someone you trust—be it a friend, family member, or mentor.

*   **Scripture Therapy:** Dive into the Bible and find stories of individuals who overcame challenges.

*   **Prayer Power:** Whenever you feel overwhelmed, take a moment to pray for strength and clarity.

Living the Faith

Taking inspiration from Abigail, Cassidy began each practice with
a prayer, assembled her team for motivational talks, and focused
on building their skills rather than lamenting over losses. Cassidy's
journey mirrored Abigail's not just in her diplomatic approach but in the
deepened connection she felt with her faith.

Journal Time!

* Write about a recent time when you felt discouraged. How did
  you handle it?

* List three qualities you admire in Abigail.

* How can you implement lessons from Abigail's story in your life?

* Think of someone who uplifts you when you're down. What makes
  their support invaluable?

Wrapping Up the Week

Discouragement is a natural part of life's ebb and flow. However, your
reaction to these low moments defines your journey. Just as Abigail found
the wisdom to navigate challenges gracefully, let her story inspire you to
find strength and wisdom in your faith, allowing you to triumph over any
discouraging situation.

Week 47: Stand Firm in Your Convictions

"Be on your guard; stand firm in the faith;
be courageous; be strong."
—1 Corinthians 16:13

> **Recommended Reading:**
> The story of Daniel (Daniel 6)

The world often tests your convictions, pushing you toward paths that might not align with your faith and values. Much like Daniel, who stood against the currents of his time, you too can stay true to yourself and your faith.

In Daniel 6, Daniel, a devout servant of God, was thrown into a den of lions because of his unwavering commitment to prayer, even when a law was passed prohibiting it. Yet, his steadfast faith protected him, and he emerged unharmed the next morning. This miraculous event demonstrates the power of staying true to one's convictions, even in the face of grave danger.

Your True Self

Peer pressure, social media trends, the desire to fit in—the modern world bombards you with endless challenges to your convictions. These challenges aren't lions, but they can be just as daunting. Maintaining a sense of self in this whirlwind is no small feat, but by anchoring yourself in faith, you can withstand these storms, just as Daniel did in the face of adversity.

Standing Firm

Keanu always had a knack for fitting in, whether it was in the classroom, on the soccer field, or during weekend hangouts. She cherished her close-knit group of friends, always relishing the laughter and shared memories. Yet, as high school progressed, Keanu began to sense a shift. The hangouts, once filled with video games and movie marathons, started to have an unfamiliar undercurrent. Just as Daniel resisted the temptation of the king's luxurious feasts, Keanu faced a contemporary challenge.

It began subtly with a shared secret look among some, which Keanu would dismiss. But soon, it was undeniable. As she walked into Jenna's dimly lit basement one evening, a cloud of sweet-scented vapor greeted her. Vaping had made its entry into her circle.

Keanu sat in an armchair, watching her friends pass around the sleek device. Each one took a drag, blowing out ornate clouds, laughing at their own dexterity. Soon, the device was being nudged toward her, its blinking light inviting her to partake.

"Come on, K," Jenna cajoled, her voice slightly breathy from her recent inhalation. "It's fun, and it's not like it's a cigarette or something."

"Yeah, just try it once," echoed Mark, "You won't get hooked or anything."

Keanu hesitated, her mind racing. She recalled her Sunday school lessons about Daniel. The parallels between his challenges and hers suddenly felt strikingly clear. She felt the weight of their expectant stares, the tension of being on the edge of a decision. Memories of their shared moments, the trust, and the camaraderie flitted through her mind. Would she jeopardize it all?

As she contemplated, a distant Sunday school memory resurfaced. It was as if the words of 1 Corinthians 16:13 echoed in her ears: "Be on your guard; stand firm in the faith." She remembered the story of Daniel, a young man in a foreign land, away from his family and community; yet, he stood unwavering in his beliefs. Daniel had faced the allure of the king's luxuries and, even more significantly, the life-threatening challenge of the lion's den. Throughout, he drew strength from his faith, standing true to his convictions, even when standing alone.

Keanu looked up, her resolve solidifying. "Thanks, guys, but I'll pass."

There was a brief pause, the background music seeming to amplify in the silence. Jenna raised an eyebrow, while Mark let out a chuckle, masking his discomfort. But Keanu's calm demeanor had shifted something. She saw Lucas, another friend, quietly pass on his turn without a word.

As the evening waned and the group dispersed, Keanu felt a mixture of emotions. The weight of potential judgment and the pride of staying true to herself battled within her. That night, she felt a kinship with Daniel that she had never felt before. As she lay in bed, she sent a silent prayer of gratitude, feeling a profound connection to a biblical figure from millennia ago.

Weeks turned into months, and while vaping remained an undercurrent, Keanu's decision started to influence subtle changes. Conversations about health risks began to surface, and a few friends, including Jenna, began questioning their choices. By senior year, the vaping device had nearly disappeared from their hangouts.

Keanu's act, inspired by a tale of faith, wasn't just about resisting a trend. It became a testament to the power of conviction. Like Daniel, her steadfastness in her beliefs influenced those around her. Years later, at a college reunion, Mark confessed, "You know, Keanu, when you said 'no' that day, it made a lot of us think. Thanks for being our Daniel."

Daily Dose of Faith

* **Stay Informed:** Understand the foundations of your beliefs. Read, research, and reflect so you can articulate and uphold your convictions.

* **Seek Supportive Company**: While it's essential to engage with diverse viewpoints, ensure you have a close circle who uplifts and supports your core values.

* **Prayerful Reflection:** Daily, spend time in prayer, seeking guidance and strength. Let the story of Daniel inspire you to remain steadfast.

* **Remember the Heroes:** Recall biblical figures like Daniel who stood firm against trials.

Living the Faith

Inspired by Daniel, Keanu decided to share her feelings with a trusted teacher. She felt that just as Daniel's faith was an example for her, she could be an example for others. The teacher started a group in school promoting healthy living, giving students a platform to discuss their challenges. Keanu became a leading voice, helping her peers navigate the pressures of life with faith and conviction.

Journal Time!

* Recall a moment when your convictions were tested. What emotions did you feel? How did you respond, and what would you do differently if faced with a similar situation again?

* What qualities in Daniel inspire you the most?

* Are there any beliefs or convictions you find challenging to uphold? Why?

* List ways you can strengthen your resolve to maintain your convictions. How can you channel the spirit of Daniel in your daily life?

Wrapping Up the Week

In a world teeming with external influences, staying true to one's convictions is a courageous act. Remember the perseverance of Daniel, and let his story be a compass when you feel your faith wavering. His tale reminds you that, with unwavering faith, you can overcome even the most daunting challenges. Stand firm, stay true, and let your convictions light your path.

Week 48: Believe in the Power of Testimony

"Let the redeemed of the Lord tell their story—
those he redeemed from the hand of the foe."
—Psalm 107:2

Recommended Reading:
The story of Shadrach, Meshach and Abednego (Daniel 3)

Every believer carries a testimony, a story of God's work in their life. Like Shadrach, Meshach, and Abednego, your testimony can influence those around you and glorify God. Just as they had the courage to stand firm in their faith, you too can be brave in sharing your personal story.

In Daniel 3, Shadrach, Meshach, and Abednego refused to bow down to King Nebuchadnezzar's golden image, staying true to their faith in the one true God. Even when threatened with a fiery furnace, they stood firm. Miraculously, God protected them from the flames. Their testimony of faith and God's deliverance became a powerful testament to all of Babylon about the mighty power of God.

Your True Self

In a world driven by perfection and the quest for external validation, your struggles and challenges are often swept under the rug, masked by a façade of contentment. However, sharing your authentic experiences—

the battles you've faced and the grace you've received—can be one of the most powerful tools of witness you possess. This is the very essence of testimony, much like Shadrach, Meshach, and Abednego's stand against the king's decree.

The Bonfire Confessions

Hannah had always been part of the in-crowd, her laughter echoing the loudest, her presence blending seamlessly. Yet, there was one distinction that set her apart—she didn't drink at parties. In a social circle where every gathering was punctuated with clinking glasses and a buzz from the booze, her choice was conspicuous. Whispers of "Why doesn't she just let loose?" and "Is she judging us?" trailed her, though they were never directly addressed.

One chilly autumn evening, as dusk melded with twilight, she found herself at Callie's backyard party. Fairy lights dangled whimsically from trees, casting a soft glow on the attendees. The centerpiece was a roaring bonfire, its flames dancing merrily, drawing people close for warmth and camaraderie. As the night wore on, drinks flowed freely, the music intensified, and the volume of laughter grew.

Yet, within the revelry, Hannah sat by the fire, nursing her cup of apple cider. It wasn't long before Liam, a longtime friend, slightly tipsy, slurred, "Come on, Hannah, just one drink. Why do you always hold back?"

The question, though not new, felt weightier under the collective, curious gaze of the group. The bonfire crackled nearby as Hannah began, "I've never shared this with you all, but I think it's time."

She took a deep breath and started talking about her cousin, Ingrid. Bright, vivacious, and life-of-the-party Ingrid who, over time, became a shadow of himself. The vibrant spark in his eyes had dulled, replaced by the hazy glint of addiction. Hannah recalled the family's anguish, the nights of whispered arguments, the days of hope followed by crushing relapses. The journey was tumultuous, but faith and a community program brought Ingrid and the family back from the brink. He found solace in spirituality, gradually piecing his life back together.

As Hannah spoke, the atmosphere palpably changed. The previously boisterous crowd had grown silent, each one engrossed, connected by the raw truth of her words. Much like how tales of unwavering faith can inspire awe, Hannah's honest words drew her friends in, resonating with their own experiences.

When she finished, there was a pause, as if the night itself held its breath. Then, softly, Ella, a vibrant cheerleader, spoke up. "I had no idea, Hannah. My brother... he struggles too." The admission seemed to break a dam, as one by one, others began sharing. Stories of personal battles, of siblings, of friends they had lost to addiction, and those still grappling.

As the night progressed and more stories were shared, the party slowly transformed. The light-hearted atmosphere gave way to one of understanding and support, much like an impromptu support group. The bonfire's warmth wasn't just physical; it became symbolic of the safety and understanding the group found in each other.

By dawn, as the fire was reduced to embers and the fairy lights dimmed, many left with a renewed sense of purpose. While not everyone changed their habits, the depth of the conversations it sparked and the bonds it strengthened were undeniable.

Weeks later, a group, led by Hannah and Ella, began meeting regularly, offering a space for sharing and healing. It wasn't about preaching or judgment; it was about understanding, compassion, and being there for one another. Their testimonies, just like those of the three men in the furnace, became a light, drawing many to its warmth and truth.

Hannah's courage to share that night didn't just break her silence; it gave voice to many hidden stories, proving that sometimes, all it takes is one spark to ignite a transformation.

Daily Dose of Faith

* **Own Your Story:** Embrace the highs and lows, for they've shaped your relationship with God.

* **Share Wisely:** Look for opportunities where your testimony can bring hope or understanding.

* **Listen Actively:** Others' testimonies can strengthen your faith. Be open to listening.

* **Seek Guidance:** Before sharing sensitive parts of your testimony, seek wisdom from trusted mentors or elders.

Living the Faith

After that night, Hannah and a few of her friends started a support group in their community, offering a safe space to share testimonies and struggles. Much like the story of Shadrach, Meshach, and Abednego had a profound impact on Babylon, these personal stories began to create waves in their community. The group grew, showcasing the ripple effect one testimony can create.

Journal Time!

* Reflect on moments in your life that felt significant or transformative. Can you articulate any of these moments as testimonies of faith or growth?

* How do the actions of Shadrach, Meshach, and Abednego inspire you?

* Are there stories or testimonies that have deeply impacted your own faith journey? Write them down.

* What fears or hesitations do you have about sharing your own testimony? Why?

Wrapping Up the Week

Your testimony, whether big or small, is a living proof of God's grace, love, and power. Embrace it. Share it. And let it bring hope to others. Just as the faith of Shadrach, Meshach, and Abednego stood as a testament to an entire kingdom, so too can your story of faith inspire and uplift those around you.

Week 49: Share Your Faith with Others

"I will tell of all your wonderful deeds."
—Psalm 9:1

> **Recommended Reading:**
> The story of Stephen (Acts 7)

It takes boldness to speak about faith, especially in environments where it might face opposition. Just as Stephen had the courage to share his beliefs, you too can share the love of Jesus, making a difference in someone's life.

In Acts 7, Stephen stands before the religious leaders, recounting Israel's history and how it points to Jesus as the Messiah. His boldness and commitment to sharing the truth, even at the cost of his life, demonstrated an unwavering faith in Christ. Because of his unwavering commitment, even in the face of extreme consequences, Stephen's story marked a pivotal moment in the early church's history.

Your True Self

Today's world often promotes self-expression, but speaking about faith can sometimes be met with skepticism or even ridicule. Stephen's courage in speaking about his faith, even in the face of adversity, is a model you can look to. Yet, deep down, the longing for purpose, acceptance, and unconditional love is universal. By sharing your faith, you could be offering someone a path to find those very things.

A Moment of Impact

Noëlle's school buzzed with excitement as "Share a Story" week began. Every student was given a chance to share a personal story, a moment that had a profound impact on their life. The auditorium was filled with the murmurs of students, hushed conversations, and occasional laughter. Teachers whispered among themselves, expectantly waiting for the next story.

She had heard about Nathan's summer in his grandparents' village, Lisa's encounter with a pod of dolphins, and Jamie's hilarious mishap during his first job at the burger joint. She had also been moved by Sarah's recounting of finding strength in prayer during a family crisis. Noëlle's palms grew sweaty as she fidgeted with the bracelet she had received during her mission trip. Every bead, every knot, every thread told a story. And it was this story she was about to share.

As her name echoed through the speakers, Noëlle felt a rush of nervousness. Recalling Stephen's fearless proclamation of faith before the Sanhedrin gave her strength. She took a deep breath, adjusting the microphone. "Last summer," she began, her voice slightly shaky, "I embarked on a mission trip to a remote village in Peru."

The screens behind her showcased photos: children with glistening eyes, elderly men and women wearing vibrant clothes, houses that bore stories of time, and the stunning landscapes. "It was more than just building houses or teaching English," Noëlle continued, her confidence growing. "It was about understanding their world, their struggles, their joys."

A particular picture caught everyone's attention: a group of village children surrounding Noëlle, all engrossed in a book. "This," she said, pointing toward it, "was the moment my perspective shifted." She spoke of Maria, a bright-eyed ten-year-old with a thirst for knowledge but limited access to books. Every evening, Noëlle would read to her under the canopy of stars.

One night, Maria curiously asked about Noëlle's bracelet, touching the cross delicately. This simple question led to profound conversations about faith, belief, and hope. "It wasn't about converting anyone," Noëlle clarified, "but about sharing how my faith grounded me and gave me purpose."

She continued, sharing snippets of moments where faith had been her anchor—dealing with academic pressures, the loss of her grandmother, and even everyday trials. "It wasn't about the big miracles," she said, "but the small, everyday moments where I felt a guiding hand, a reassuring presence."

"Just as Stephen shared the wonders of God's deeds in the past, I found strength in sharing my own personal journey with God," Noëlle voiced toward the end.

Noëlle finished her story with a powerful statement, "Each bead in this bracelet signifies a step in my faith journey, whether it's a lesson learned, a soul touched, or an emotion experienced. It symbolizes my journey, not just in Peru, but my journey of faith."

As she stepped down, the applause was genuine and heartfelt. But what struck Noëlle most was the queue of classmates waiting to talk to her. Some shared their stories, some inquired about the mission trip, while others expressed an interest in understanding her faith more deeply.

Ethan, who was known more for his prowess on the basketball court than his spiritual inclinations, admitted he'd never given much thought to spirituality but felt inspired to explore it. Lucy, a shy girl from Noëlle's English class, shared how she'd faced challenges with her family and was searching for something to believe in.

Days after her speech, Noëlle found herself in new conversations, surrounded by diverse voices, all eager to understand, learn, and share. She realized that while her mission trip was about helping a village in Peru, it also paved the way for a new mission in her school: bridging connections and fostering understanding through shared stories.

Daily Dose of Faith

* **Lead with Love:** Before sharing your beliefs, show genuine care and love toward others.

* **Know Your Story:** Reflect on your journey with God, so you can share genuinely.

* **Ask Questions:** Engage others by understanding their beliefs and perspectives.

* **Stay Humble:** Remember it's about God's love, not winning an argument.

Living the Faith

Inspired by her "Share a Story" experience, Noëlle began a faith-based club at school. They met weekly to discuss their experiences, answer questions, and support each other. The club became a sanctuary for many seeking answers.

Journal Time!

* Have you ever shared your faith with someone? What was the experience like?

* How does Stephen's story inspire or challenge you?

* What are some ways you can authentically share your faith in your daily life?

* Are there areas or situations where you find it difficult to talk about your faith? Why?

Wrapping Up the Week

Sharing your faith story can inspire, comfort, and guide those around you. Like Stephen, who stood before a hostile crowd, sharing the message of salvation, your testimony can inspire hope to those searching for meaning. Be bold, be kind, and let God's love shine through your words and actions.

Week 50: Invest in Eternity

"Do not store up for yourselves treasures on earth, where moths and vermin destroy, and where thieves break in and steal. But store up for yourselves treasures in heaven, where moths and vermin do not destroy, and where thieves do not break in and steal."

—Matthew 6:19–20

Recommended Reading:
The story of the poor widow (Mark 12)

Life presents countless choices on where to invest your time, energy, and resources. The story of the poor widow teaches you that investments are about intention, not just quantity. Just as she valued eternal treasures over earthly wealth, you too are called to prioritize lasting investments.

In Mark 12, among wealthy donors, a poor widow dropped two small coins into the temple treasury. While her contribution seemed insignificant in comparison, Jesus commended her, saying she gave all she had to live on. It wasn't about the amount but about her heart's sacrifice. This act is a timeless lesson on understanding the essence of genuine giving.

Your True Self

With the constant influence of social media and peer pressure, it's tempting to chase fleeting pleasures and validations. However, as the widow revealed, the world often overlooks the true depth of your investments. But true value and legacy lie in investing in things that have lasting impact, both in this world and in eternity.

The Dress and the Decision

Cassie's eyes were fixed on the designer dress she had bookmarked on her laptop. Just like the widow who stood with those giving much, Cassie too stood on the brink of a profound decision. Every detail of it seemed perfect—the subtle shimmer, the intricate embroidery, the way it gracefully fell to the floor. Cassie could already imagine herself dancing in it at the upcoming senior prom.

For months, Cassie had undertaken odd jobs after school—babysitting, tutoring younger kids, even helping out at the local café during the weekends. Every time she received her pay, she'd meticulously transfer the majority to her "Dress Fund," feeling a flutter of excitement. The day she had enough was so close she could almost touch it.

One evening, at her youth group gathering, Pastor Mike made an announcement. They were planning a mission trip to a neighboring state where a community had been adversely affected by recent floods. The group intended to help rebuild homes and provide essential supplies. It was a chance to make a tangible difference.

Cassie's close friend, Lila, sat next to her with a face mixed with hope and resignation. Lila had always been passionate about community service, but Cassie knew her family had been going through financial hardships.

"I wish I could go," Lila whispered, a hint of sorrow in her voice. "But with everything at home... I just can't afford the trip."

The room was filled with the excited chatter of those already planning the logistics, but Cassie's mind raced elsewhere. A thought began to form, one that wrestled with her long-held dream of the designer dress. That night, as Cassie lay in bed, she held an internal debate.

The dress was a symbol of her hard work and dreams, but the mission trip presented an opportunity for a different kind of fulfillment.

Two days later, with a deep breath, Cassie approached Lila. "I want to sponsor you for the trip," she said hesitantly. Lila stared at her, eyes wide in disbelief.

"Cassie, that's your Dress Fund," Lila protested. "You've worked so hard for it!"

Cassie smiled, her decision solidifying. "It's just a dress, Lila. Seeing you make a difference, helping those people—that's worth more." In that moment, Cassie reflected the essence of the poor widow's giving, choosing lasting impact over temporary pleasure.

The gratitude and sheer joy in Lila's eyes was a sight Cassie would never forget. The happiness radiated, warming both Lila and Cassie.

Weeks later, photos from the mission trip showed Lila with muddy jeans, messy hair, but brilliant eyes. She had traded temporary treasures for eternal joys, much like the message in Matthew's gospel. She was surrounded by grateful families, children clinging to her, their faces lit up with laughter.

On prom night, Cassie wore a simple dress she found on sale. It didn't have the designer tag or the intricate embroidery, but she wore it with pride. As she danced, she felt a joy deeper than any material possession could offer.

The designer dress would have been a fleeting memory, a short-lived dream. But the decision to forgo it created memories that would last a lifetime—of selflessness, of deep friendship, and of understanding the true value of sacrifices.

Daily Dose of Faith

* **Value Intent:** It's not about how much you give, but the love and intention behind it.

* **Seek Eternal Rewards:** Material things fade, but spiritual investments last forever.

* **Pray for Guidance:** Ask God to guide your decisions, ensuring they align with His purpose.

* **Generosity of Heart:** Give freely, not out of obligation but out of genuine love.

Living the Faith

Cassie's choice inspired others in her youth group, leading to a wave of generosity and kindness. Many started fundraising, others donated their talents, and some shared stories that brought awareness. It was a testament to the ripple effects that true, heartfelt investments can create, just as the widow's meager offering left an everlasting impact.

Journal Time!

* Think about a meaningful gift you've given. How did that experience make you feel?

* What are some ways you can invest in eternal things?

* How do you balance the pressures of the world with the calling to invest in what lasts?

* Think about someone who embodies the spirit of the poor widow. What can you learn from them?

Wrapping Up the Week

Your choices today mold your legacy for eternity. Cassie's sacrifice, reminiscent of the poor widow's, serves as a reminder that sometimes the smallest gestures can have the most profound impacts. While the world offers fleeting pleasures, investing in eternal causes provides profound, lasting fulfillment. Like the poor widow, may you learn the power of sacrificial giving and the joy of investing in what truly matters.

Week 51: Celebrate God's Faithfulness

"Give thanks to the Lord, for he is good;
his love endures forever."
—1 Chronicles 16:34

Recommended Reading:
The story of Ruth (Ruth 1:16–17; 2:2–3; 4:13–17)

Life is a journey, marked by milestones of challenges, joys, hardships, and victories. Through every twist and turn, God's faithfulness remains a constant. Just as Ruth faced uncertainty and chose loyalty, you too are often confronted with decisions that challenge your faith. The story of Ruth beautifully illustrates the depth of God's loyalty to those who trust in Him.

Ruth, originally from Moab, became a widow and faced a choice. She chose loyalty to her bereaved mother-in-law, Naomi, and embraced faith in the God of Israel, setting forth on a journey to a foreign land. Despite facing potential poverty and obscurity, she worked diligently and honored Naomi. Ruth's faith was rewarded when she was integrated into the community and became the great-grandmother of King David. Her story is a testament to God's faithfulness to those who remain steadfast.

Your True Self

In a world filled with fleeting trends and shifting loyalties, it's easy to feel lost or forsaken. Much like Ruth felt in a foreign land, your journey can be daunting. But in the noise and chaos, there's a steadfast anchor—God's unwavering faithfulness. No matter how the world may change, His love and promises remain.

Legacy of Resilience

Lorelei's once tidy room was now in disarray—notebooks strewn across the floor, clothes piled on the chair, signs of a mind burdened and distracted. Just as Ruth faced an uncertain future after the death of her husband, Lorelei too was grappling with a new reality. The announcement of her parents' divorce had split her life into a "before" and an "after." The once bubbly teenager was now often caught staring into the distance, the weight of the world seemingly on her shoulders.

The quiet of the weekend was interrupted by the soft creaking of her door. Just as Naomi offered solace to Ruth, Uncle Thedric peeked in, his silver hair cut short, holding a worn leather-bound journal. "Thought you might find some comfort in this," he said, placing it beside Lorelei.

With a quizzical look, Lorelei opened the journal. The pages, though yellowed with age, held stories penned with love and care. It was a chronicle of their family history, tracing back to generations.

One entry spoke of a great-great-grandmother, Heidi, who had journeyed across the seas as a young bride, clinging onto her faith during tumultuous times. Another was about Aunt Zelda, who had lost her husband during the war, raising three kids alone with unfaltering grace. Like Ruth who gleaned hope from her faith and the kindness of Boaz, Lorelei found solace in the stories of her ancestors. Every tale was woven with threads of perseverance, strength, and reliance on faith.

As Lorelei turned the pages, she stumbled upon a passage someone had highlighted: "In times of sorrow, I look to the story of Ruth. Despite her losses and uncertainty, she trusted in God's plan, finding solace

244

and strength. Her story reminds me that even in our brokenness, God's faithfulness remains."

With every tale, Lorelei felt a warmth enveloping her—a sense of belonging, a realization that she was part of a legacy of formidable women who had faced heartaches and challenges but emerged stronger. These women weren't just characters in a journal; they were a testament to resilience, determination, and unwavering faith.

One evening, Lorelei sat down with Uncle Thedric, the journal between them. "It's strange," Lorelei began, her voice soft, "how their stories from decades ago seem so relevant to me now."

Uncle Thedric smiled gently. "Ruth's unwavering faith in trying times inspires many across generations," he said. "Hardships are a part of life. But these stories show that with faith, you can find a way to navigate them. Just like Ruth, each woman in our family has leaned on God during her toughest times."

Lorelei sighed. "It's just... I feel lost. But reading about them... It gives me hope."

"You're part of this lineage, Lorelei," her uncle reassured, "Their strength, their faith—it runs in your veins too."

The weeks that followed saw a subtle change in Lorelei. The journal had become her anchor. In Ruth's story, she saw a reflection of her own journey, reminding her that God's love is steadfast. Through stories of the past, Lorelei found hope for her future—a hope rooted in faith, family, and the resilience of the women who came before her. It became therapeutic—a place not just to vent, but to draw strength.

One day, she wrote, "Like Ruth, I'm in a chapter of uncertainty. But I'm not alone. I have the lessons of these remarkable women and my unyielding faith. This too shall pass."

The divorce had created a chasm in Lorelei's life, but the journal bridged it, reminding her of her legacy. Through stories of the past, Lorelei found hope for her future—a hope rooted in faith, family, and the resilience of the women who came before her.

Daily Dose of Faith

* **Recognize God's Presence:** In both the highs and lows, see God's hand guiding and protecting you.

* **Celebrate Small Victories:** Acknowledge everyday blessings as a testament to God's faithfulness.

* **Share Stories:** Talk about moments when you felt God's presence, reinforcing His constancy.

* **Trust the Process:** Like Ruth, know that God has a plan, even if it's not immediately clear.

Living the Faith

Drawing inspiration from the women in her family, Lorelei started a gratitude journal, writing daily about moments where she felt God's faithfulness. Emulating Ruth's steadfastness, this practice anchored her in recognizing God's hand, not only strengthening her faith but also encouraging her friends to seek and recognize God's hand in their own lives.

Journal Time!

* When have you felt God's faithfulness in your life?

* What lessons can you draw from Ruth's loyalty and determination?

* How can you cultivate a daily habit of recognizing God's hand in your life?

* Think of ways you can celebrate and share God's faithfulness with others.

Wrapping Up the Week

Ruth's story is a testament that even in the face of adversity, loyalty and trust in God can pave the way to unimaginable blessings. You too can find hope and strength in the unwavering faithfulness of the Lord. Ruth's story is more than just a tale from ancient times; it's a living testimony of God's enduring faithfulness. By recognizing and celebrating God's unwavering love, you can strengthen your faith, serve as a pillar of hope for others, and carry forward the legacy of trust, just as Ruth did. As Lorelei discovered, your lineage of faith is a chain, each link made stronger by tales of God's unwavering love.

Week 52: Step into Your Future with Confidence

"I can do all things through Christ who gives me strength."
—Philippians 4:13

> **Recommended Reading:**
> The story of Joseph (Genesis 37:3–5, 23–28)

As you approach a new chapter in your life, uncertainties may arise. But, equipped with faith, you can stride into your future with confidence, understanding that God has a divine blueprint for you, much like He did for Hagar.

Hagar found herself wandering in the wilderness, cast out and forsaken by her mistress Sarah. With her child, she faced the bleakness of the desert and the haunting uncertainty of the future. Yet, in her moment of deepest despair, God appeared to her, assuring her of His presence and the great destiny of her son, Ishmael. Through it all, Hagar realized that she was seen and known by the Almighty.

Your True Self

Your journey is riddled with changes, questions, and self-discovery. It's natural to sometimes feel swamped by doubts and fears. Yet, within you lies the power to rise, anchored by God's promises and guided by His providence. As Hagar faced her trials, you too can find the strength to confront your own adversities with faith and perseverance.

A Melody Through Adversity

Avery had always possessed a voice that could enchant listeners. As a child, she'd belt out tunes, turning their modest living room into a concert hall. She dreamed of grand stages, with lights that shone as brightly as her ambitions. However, as the years went by, the universe seemed to be playing a different tune.

At school, classmates would mockingly whisper, "Avery, the superstar!" with exaggerated bows. Each sneer seemed to chip away at her confidence. "Maybe they're right," she thought one evening, cradling her guitar, "Perhaps I'm chasing a fantasy."

The echo of laughter and doubt reverberated louder each day, and Avery found herself retreating from her dream. In times of trial, it can be comforting to remember figures like Hagar, who also faced despair and isolation. She began avoiding any conversation about her music and hid her songbooks, as if concealing evidence of a crime. The haunting weight of what-ifs and the shadow of failure loomed, and Avery was on the verge of resigning her dreams to a dusty corner.

One chilly evening, while trying to distract herself, Avery happened upon the tale of Hagar in an old family Bible. The similarity struck her. Just as Hagar had faced rejection and found herself alone in the wilderness, Avery too faced isolation and doubt. A woman, forsaken and left to fend for herself, yet comforted and guided by God.

Hagar's story wasn't just about her hardships; it was about her resilience, her faith, and the profound realization that she was seen by God. Avery felt an immediate connection. Just as Hagar's time in the desert was not the end but a moment of divine intervention, Avery realized hardships were merely setups for greater blessings.

"Am I not seen?" she reflected, finding solace in the idea that she too was under God's watchful eye.

Encouraged by Hagar's tenacity and God's presence in her story, Avery reignited her passion. She now understood that setbacks were not denials but mere challenges pushing her forward. Each setback became an inspiration, driving her to pursue her dreams with even greater zeal.

Wanting to share the depth of her journey and faith, Avery began to upload her renditions online. The soul she infused into her music was palpable. People began to notice, share, and soon enough, her voice was touching hearts across the globe. Where once mockery shadowed Avery's past, now applause illuminated her present.

One evening, while performing at a local café, a producer from a renowned music label approached her. "Your voice," he began, "it feels like it's been through a journey. It's raw, real. We'd love to have you on board."

Tears welled up in Avery's eyes. "It has been a journey," she whispered.

Years later, as she took the stage, with thousands chanting her name, Avery's past flashed before her eyes—the sneers, the self-doubt, and that fateful evening with Joseph's story. As the music began, she sang not just with her voice, but with her heart and soul, echoing the trials, tribulations, and triumphs of her journey.

Avery had once almost allowed her dreams to be buried under mockery and doubt. Yet, inspired by a tale from the past, she had risen, understanding that sometimes, the darkest pits lead to the most dazzling palaces.

Daily Dose of Faith

* **Affirm Your Worth:** God created you with purpose and value.

* **Visualize Your Success:** Remind yourself of figures like Hagar, who found strength even in desolation. Envision yourself achieving your goals under God's watchful eye.

- * **Seek Mentorship:** Connect with positive role models who can share wisdom and encouragement.
- * **Pray for Guidance:** Regularly consult God about your path, trusting in His plans for you.

Living the Faith

Inspired by Hagar's story, Avery started attending vocal classes. She surrounded herself with positive mentors and sought opportunities, not just to sing, but to touch hearts with her voice. As Hagar felt God's guidance during her trials, Avery felt His divine touch on every note she sang. Each performance was a testament to her faith and perseverance.

Journal Time!

- * What dreams do you harbor in your heart?
- * Have there been moments of doubt or setbacks? How did you handle them?
- * Reflecting on Hagar's story, how can you see your current challenges as stepping stones?
- * As you look ahead, what steps can you take to step into your future confidently?

Wrapping Up the Week

Much like Hagar's story, your life is an intricate masterpiece where every element, whether joy, sorrow, victory, or setback, contributes to the overall picture. As you step into the future, know that you walk with the God who guided Hagar through her wilderness. Embrace your journey with faith, and step into your future with confidence.

Conclusion

What a Ride
It's Been!

From your first steps together in this faith-filled voyage to now, you've embarked on a transformative journey of heart, soul, and purpose. Through *Radiant Faith*, I've been honored to share pieces of my heart and the stories I've collected. And in doing so, I hope I've been able to illuminate parts of your own story.

Life has a peculiar way of intertwining challenges with blessings. Times of doubt may pave the way for unwavering belief, and moments of despair can lead to profound hope. Just as I found solace and strength during the chaos of my youth, my sincere wish is that *Radiant Faith* has provided you with similar refuge and encouragement.

Your journey with faith doesn't end here. Instead, consider this a launchpad, an invigorating start to a continuous exploration with God by your side. Embrace your radiant faith and carry forward the lessons. Your relationship with God is as unique as you are.

I'd like to leave you with a sentiment that has carried me through my darkest nights and brightest days: Your faith, no matter how small or grand, has the power to not only illuminate your path but to brighten the world around you.

So, keep shining, dear traveler. With every trial and triumph, let your faith be your guide. Although our shared journey in these pages concludes, the adventure of faith is ever-evolving, endlessly inspiring, and eternally radiant.

Until our paths cross again, may God's blessings and boundless love surround you. Here's to the continuation of your radiant journey!

With all my heart,
M.J. Fievre

About the Author

M.J. Fievre, BS Ed, is a devoted Christian writer and educator who has dedicated her life to guiding and inspiring teens on their spiritual journey. Born and raised in a Christian household, she received her foundational education at the Catholic school, Sainte Rose de Lima. During her time there, M.J. engaged in in-depth Bible studies, fostering a deep understanding of Christian teachings. As a leader of "Jeunesse Mariale," a Catholic youth movement in Port-au-Prince, she mentored her peers, helping them to deepen their understanding of Christianity and fuel their spiritual growth. Continuing her spiritual education, M.J. attended Notre Dame of Haiti in Port-au-Prince and later transferred to Barry University, both Catholic institutions. Her dedication to her faith and community is evident through her active involvement in her church's dream team, where she serves in the children's program. Her extensive experience in faith-based education, service, and her background as an accomplished author with a strong track record in sales make her the ideal choice for crafting a devotional guide like *Radiant Faith*. Through this book, M.J. aims to inspire and empower young women to deepen their spiritual connection and navigate the challenges they face daily. She lives in Winter Garden, Florida.

Mango Publishing, established in 2014, publishes an eclectic list of books by diverse authors—both new and established voices—on topics ranging from business, personal growth, women's empowerment, LGBTQ studies, health, and spirituality, to history, popular culture, time management, decluttering, lifestyle, mental wellness, aging, and sustainable living. We were named 2019 *and* 2020's #1 fastest growing independent publisher by *Publishers Weekly*. Our success is driven by our main goal, which is to publish high-quality books that will entertain readers as well as make a positive difference in their lives.

Our readers are our most important resource; we value your input, suggestions, and ideas. We'd love to hear from you—after all, we are publishing books for you!

Please stay in touch with us and follow us at:

Facebook: Mango Publishing
Twitter: @MangoPublishing
Instagram: @MangoPublishing
LinkedIn: Mango Publishing
Pinterest: Mango Publishing
Newsletter: mangopublishinggroup.com/newsletter

Join us on Mango's journey to reinvent publishing, one book at a time.

Printed in the USA
CPSIA information can be obtained
at www.ICGtesting.com
JSHW032350041223
53181JS00006B/9

9 781684 813933